MEN FOR THE MINISTRY

Men for the Ministry

THE HISTORY OF
THE LONDON COLLEGE OF DIVINITY

G. C. B. DAVIES

Canon Treasurer of St. Patrick's Cathedral, Dublin
Professor of Ecclesiastical History and of Pastoral Theology,
Trinity College, Dublin

With a Foreword by
The Bishop of London

HODDER AND STOUGHTON

Printed by The Camelot Press Ltd., London and Southampton, for
Hodder and Stoughton Ltd., St. Paul's House,
Warwick Square, London, E.C.4.

FOREWORD

AT a time when the Church of England is giving most anxious thought to the related problems of recruitment and training for the Ministry, it is not only interesting but heartening to read of the efforts made a century ago to supply the Church's need for clergy. The period between 1840 and 1870 was one of great developments in the life and work of the Church. During that time most of our Theological Colleges and Teacher Training Colleges were founded and built by the generosity of Church people, and at the same time church schools of every type were built and a vast number of new parishes came into being.

This history of the London College of Divinity is a welcome addition to our knowledge and understanding of this great period in our Church's life. The foundations of faith seemed to be attacked from without by men like Darwin, whose *Origin of Species* was published in 1859, and from within by such unorthodox views as were expressed in *Essays and Reviews* in 1860. At a time when ordinands were most needed they seemed reluctant to come forward—and, as Professor Davies so well shows, the same opinions on recruitment and training were expressed as we have heard in recent years.

Alfred Peache founded the London College of Divinity to help to meet the needs of his day. This history tells us how the College responded to that challenge and to the changing needs of the Church over the hundred years of its history. It tells us, too, of the agonising debates on the need to leave Highbury and on the choice of a new site. Now in its new and splendid home at Northwood the College is strong and flourishing and faces the future with a confidence which this centenary record will enhance.

ROBERT LONDIN.

AUTHOR'S PREFACE

I WAS greatly honoured by the Council's invitation to write the history of the College. Owing to other commitments, and living at a distance from my principal sources of material, the task would have been impossible but for the most generous assistance from many who were interested in the project.

My first and deepest expression of gratitude must be extended to the Principal, the Rev. Hugh Jordan, who, despite the pressure of his own work, offered me most welcome hospitality on the numerous, and at times inconvenient, occasions when I descended upon the College, wrote almost a volume of letters on my behalf to obtain necessary information, and arranged for the photographing of the illustrations. I am also indebted to him for the suggestion of the title. The other members of the staff, including the Lady Housekeeper, Miss Redfern, and the College Secretary, Miss Millard, tolerated my visits with commendable forbearance, in view of the additional work which was inevitably involved.

My thanks are due to all those who sent in memoranda, and in particular to His Grace the Archbishop of York, who gathered much initial material, and read through the typescript; his interest and informed criticism were of the utmost value at every stage of the work. The Rev. Martin Parsons also helped me with suggestions and information.

Finally, I should like to thank the Bishop of London, the College Visitor, for most kindly consenting to write the Foreword, and Leonard Cutts, Esq., of Messrs Hodder and Stoughton, for much technical assistance and information.

G. C. B. D.

"BIRNAM,"
CABINTEELY,
CO. DUBLIN.

CONTENTS

LIST OF ILLUSTRATIONS

*The first group of illustrations follow page 64
and the second group follow page 80*

PART I

The History of the College

CHAPTER I

Foundation and Development, 1863–84

DURING 1957, a casual passer-by would have noticed considerable activity in an area named Broad Oak Field, near the junction of Green Lane and Rickmansworth Road at Northwood. Some large red-brick buildings were in course of erection, set well back from the road, and his enquiries would have revealed that this was to be a theological college, with chapel, dining-hall, library, lecture-rooms and living accommodation for some fifty students and staff. It was the London College of Divinity, he would have been told; but if his curiosity had been further aroused to ask whether this was the foundation of a new college or a new location for an old one, few of the workmen employed would have been able to give him much further information, except, perhaps, a vague reference to a place called Highbury.

For the time being, Northwood fades out of the picture, as we go back almost a hundred years before those days of building activity, to the mid-Victorian era. In 1859, heads were being shaken over the publication of a work by a certain Charles Darwin, entitled *The Origin of Species*, which, in the opinion of some, appeared to attack the very foundations of Christianity. As if this were not bad enough, from within the Church came a volume in 1860 entitled *Essays and Reviews*, which roused to wrath sober-minded men, who were bewildered by the expression of such unorthodox opinions. What was the Church coming to? And what kind of young men were coming forward to be ordained in this age of doubt and questioning? The same questions were being asked by those whose duty it was to supervise such men at this time, as the following quotation makes clear:

"Whatever the causes may be, the facts lie beyond dispute. Young men, even those of zeal and piety, hesitate to come forward. . . . Thus the Church of England is in a fair way, if no remedy can be found for a state of things becoming daily worse, to sink into premature decay for the want of ministers

15

to officiate in her churches. Two questions confront us ... first, how is this deficiency to be explained? And next, what steps can be taken for its removal?"

The writer continued: "Amongst remedial measures, search [should be made] for candidates in a wider field," such as "the families of the mercantile community and the higher class of tradesman," that is to say, amongst those who had had no university education. It might be thought that these words were written in fairly modern times, but in fact as already stated they appeared in an article in a Church periodical of a century ago.[1] The lack of candidates for the ministry, and the best methods by which they might be trained, were exercising the minds of ecclesiastical authorities then as now, and the history of the London College of Divinity is an attempt to answer one of the questions posed, while it also traces the adoption of one of the suggestions made by the writer of this article.

The college owes its foundation and early development to a partnership between two men of vision, ability and determination: Alfred Peache and Thomas Pownall Boultbee. Alfred Peache was the son of James Courthope Peache, a business-man living in Wimbledon. He had two sons: Clement, the elder, and Alfred, and an only daughter, Kezia. Alfred was born in 1818, and graduated in 1842 from Wadham College, Oxford. Mr. Peache, Senior, was said to have been much averse to his son's determination to take Holy Orders, but Alfred, having made his choice, began to study, at the same time helping in parochial work under Mr. Brodie, Vicar of Mangotsfield and Downend, the latter a developing suburb of Bristol. Mr. Peache was ordained and licensed to the curacy of this parish in 1842 by Dr. Monck, the first Bishop of the united sees of Gloucester and Bristol. Here he lived, before his marriage, with his sister Kezia, remaining until 1854, when he became curate of Heckfield, Hampshire, for five years. In 1857 his father died suddenly, leaving Alfred and Kezia the possessors of very considerable wealth. If the young curate had now transplanted himself and his family from Heckfield to Wimbledon, and set up house in the mansion intended by his father's will for his mother, sister and brother, "with carriages, horses, cows, wines, liquors, provisions, etc.," the world would not have been surprised. But Alfred Peache was of sterner stuff. His father had bequeathed to him the advowson of Mangotsfield, and within a few months his first Vicar, Brodie, died. Peache at once succeeded him as incumbent, and before long was looking for a wider outlet for service than parochial work. Through

[1] *Christian Observer*, January, 1864, p. 55.

16

Mr. Brodie, he already knew a neighbouring clergyman, the Rev. Joseph Ditcher, Vicar of South Brent, Somersetshire, a prominent Evangelical. He had become well known through being involved in a famous ritual case in 1856 with Archdeacon G. A. Denison of Taunton, a noted High Churchman, who had preached some controversial sermons in Wells Cathedral in 1853 and 1854 on the doctrine of the Real Presence, and had fallen foul of his diocesan, Bishop Bagot. Under instructions from the Evangelical Alliance, Ditcher prosecuted in Archbishop Sumner's court; proceedings were transferred to the Court of Queen's Bench, as a result of which Denison was deprived. It was Ditcher who suggested to Peache that it was most desirable that a definitely Evangelical Theological College should be founded to train men for the ministry. Peache was greatly attracted by this idea, and, after discussing the matter with his sister, he determined to establish a London College of Divinity, at an initial outlay of fifty thousand pounds. They accordingly executed an indenture, dated July 27th, 1863, to found such a College, the fundamental principle of which is contained in this extract from its Trust Dead:

> "The teaching and government shall always be strictly Protestant and Evangelical, in conformity with the doctrines of the United Church of England and Ireland, as expressed in the Thirty-Nine Articles, as now by law established, interpreted according to the plain and natural meaning thereof."

The money being now dedicated for this use, it remained to find a Principal. Peache discussed the matter with Dr. Francis Close, Rector of Cheltenham (later Dean of Carlisle), who suggested a former curate of his, the Rev. Thomas Pownall Boultbee, from 1852 divinity lecturer and chaplain of Cheltenham College under Dr. Barry, later Principal of King's College, London, and afterwards Bishop of Sydney. Apparently Peache and Boultbee were already known to each other, for there is reason to think that in 1860 Boultbee had read a paper before the Western Clerical and Lay Association at which Peache was present, calling attention to the urgent need for an Evangelical Theological College.[1] He was the son of the Rev. Thomas Boultbee, for forty-seven years Vicar of Bidford, near Stratford-upon-Avon. The son was born on August 7th, 1818, and was educated at Uppingham, where, it is stated, he showed his strength of character (or was it prudence?) by refusing to join in a rebellion. He was deeply influenced by his mother, and at school read those Scripture portions which she had arranged

[1] See G. R. Balleine, *History of the Evangelical Party*, p. 275.

for him. He remarked in after years, "I little know how much I am indebted to my mother's prayers." He went up with an exhibition to St. John's College, Cambridge, taking his degree of B.A. in 1841 as fifth Wrangler. He was third in the Smith's prizeman examination for mathematics, and was elected to a College fellowship, being ordained by the Bishop of Ely in 1844. He resigned his fellowship on his marriage in 1846, and soon after became curate to the Rev. Francis Close at Cheltenham. Boultbee now accepted Peache's offer, and so became the first Principal. Dean Close exercised a strong influence on Boultbee at a formative stage in his career,[1] (do not impressions gained in first curacies remain with us for life?), and it was not surprising that when Peache was looking for a Principal of his new college, Boultbee should have been recommended.

Temporary premises, built for a school and known as St. John's Hall, were rented in St. John's Wood, near Kilburn Station, and there the new College unobtrusively commenced its career. The name, being also that of Boultbee's old college, has always been retained. We turn with interest to the reminiscences of Mrs. Boultbee, recorded nearly forty years afterwards. It was on August 8th, 1863, that she and her husband came from Cheltenham, and made their home in London.

> "Correspondence was going on with a few men who were thinking of entering the college. The first accepted was Thomas Lewthwaite: the first to enter was James Francis Browne, who came into residence on November 23rd. He was alone until the Christmas vacation. I may just say of him that he was a comfort to my husband as senior student at the beginning of the work: the son of a Naval officer, and at sea himself until he decided to take the step of preparing for ordination, and therefore used to discipline and order, he was afterwards Archdeacon of Madras. On January 20th, 1864, the College re-opened with six students. More were applying, and on March 3rd [1864] at a meeting of the Council, they decided to rent a house in Greville [*sic*; actually Mortimer] Road back to back with ours, making a temporary passage across, and so using them together, with steps and planks over the dividing wall."

Meanwhile, Mr. Peache went forward in gathering together a College Council, and Governing Body. The first President was the great philanthropist Lord Shaftesbury, K.G.: the honorary treasurer, the Hon. Arthur Kinnaird, M.P., later Lord Kinnaird; and the following were members of the original Council: The Rev. Alfred Peache, the Revs. Joseph Ditcher, Robert Conway (Canon of Westminster and

---

[1] Close and Boultbee remained intimate friends until the Dean's death in 1882.

Rector of St. Margaret's), Canon R. Burgess of Chelsea: and among laymen, Captain the Hon. Francis Maude, R.N., and Messrs. Alexander Haldane, Editor of the *Record*, and Robert Baxter, a noted Parliamentary lawyer; while the first Honorary Secretary was W. Irving Hare.

For the first term, then, the College consisted of one Principal and one student, and "lectures" were a dialogue between teacher and taught. But during 1864 the one student multiplied tenfold, and among new members were Thomas Lewthwaite, Henry Martin, Frederick Anderson, Robert Handcock, Lewis Sanders, two others who did not become ordained, and Francis Newton, who was the first student from the new College to take the B.A. degree of London University. Under the care and guidance of the Principal and Mrs. Boultbee, the new institution (according to one student) rather "resembled a large private family than a place of academical instruction."

The Principal's first report to the Council was in March, 1864. There had been altogether seventeen applications, drawn from very varied backgrounds; three were sons of clergymen, one of a naval officer, one was being trained for the medical profession. Of those from commercial life, two had been employed as Scripture readers. Their educational attainments were not high, and their knowledge of the Bible limited. On the other hand, Boultbee could speak with the greatest confidence of their personal piety: "None have been admitted without solid testimony reaching back for several years to the reality of the work of grace in them." Two candidates had been sent from the Clerical Education Aid Society, which paid their expenses. Three examiners of candidates for admission were appointed by the Council, the Revs. J. Patteson, C. D. Marston and R. Burgess. The Principal recommended that the examiners of the Clerical Education Aid Society should also be appointed examiners of the new College: "Their practice is identical with our own, and it is not desirable to multiply examinations of this kind for candidates."

Boultbee was troubled as to the academic standard required on entrance; if a case appeared unsatisfactory in this respect, had he the power to reject him on his own initiative? Would this procedure bring him into collision with friends of the College? Again, if the examiners disagreed (as had already happened in one case), who should make the final decision? Unfortunately, the answers given by the Council to these queries are not known, but probably a good deal was left to Boultbee's discretion. The upper age limit for admission had been fixed at twenty-seven, but Boultbee requested permission to admit older men; how should he deal with a suitable candidate who brought a promise of ordination from a bishop provided he made satisfactory use of his time at the College? Another point calling for immediate attention was the long-term policy for the future of the College. Already, space was completely filled; it would not do for the idea to get abroad that this was a small private institution, with neither library nor lecture room. As regards teaching staff, while he could manage alone at the moment, if he should divide the men into classes, further assistance would be needed. In this case, he would look for—

"a young man of piety and sound scholarship, who would take an interest in his duties and thoroughly work up the fundamental grammatical and other deficiencies in the new students. It would be very important that he should have rooms in College and be present at all the meals. It would be an advantage to the students to have him easily accessible and he might aid materially in forming a good tone of thought and manners."

Boultbee also desired information as to the Council's views on which poor districts would provide opportunities for the men to do pastoral work; should singing and elocution instruction be given; what vacations should be arranged; the appointment of a medical officer; the nature of the matriculation examination to be arranged for each student to take after six months' residence—should all take the same examination, whatever their entrance standards had been? What was the College's position in relation to the bishops? Finally, and above all, he stressed the absolute necessity to provide a library, without which the College would become before long an object of ridicule.

From this it will be obvious that a formidable list of problems confronted the Council, and the new Principal, but they were by no means dismayed. By the time of the Principal's second report, probably in June, 1864, the building was full to overflowing with nine students. These required much individual attention. In response to a circular sent out appealing for books for the library some 300 had been contributed. Pencilled comments at the end of the report indicate that Boultbee was authorised to pay £100 stipend per annum for an unordained tutor; or up to £150 per annum with board and lodgings for an ordained man, the latter being preferred. In June, 1865, he reported the appointment of the Rev. Charles Henry Waller, B.A., of University College, Oxford, who had been warmly commended by the Rev. A. M. W. Christopher of St. Aldate's, Oxford, "on the grounds of decided piety, doctrinal soundness, accurate scholarship, genial nature, and attractive manner with young men." He had also been recommended by the Rev. W. Pennefather, to whom he had been curate at St. Jude's, Mildmay Park. As to the students, Boultbee reported continuing satisfactory progress; and, looking forward to the time for examinations, he believed that, far from lowering the standard of clerical attainment, it would rather be raised through the successful completion of the College course. He went on to commend the course for the London University degree, and expressed the hope that those who arrived with a sufficiently high academic standard should be entered for this degree, and so leave their College (he added, with a touch of wry humour) "with whatever guarantee for learning the letters B.A. after their name may imply." The library had now expanded to 1,500 volumes, but certain important books were lacking, such as Alford's Greek Testament. As to other works, he wished to subscribe to Clark's Foreign Theological Library, which published English translations of the best German divines "who have met and defeated Neology in its birthplace." As a result of this report, an elocution teacher was recommended, while he and Canon Burgess were nominated to meet Dr. Jelf, of King's College, London, to discuss the question of having the same examiners.

The Principal and Tutor now shared between them lectures in Classics, a certain amount of mathematics, history, Old and New Testament, Hebrew (for second-year students) and liturgy. Parochial work in the neighbourhood was provided by several incumbents; it included Sunday School and Ragged School teaching. Only a few men came to the college straight from school. The Principal preferred men in their early twenties who, as he said, "had pricked some of the bubbles of life."

At this point, it may be well to look at the impressions of one or two early students of the new foundation. Thomas Lewthwaite has described in considerable detail the difficulty that he experienced in finding the College at all on an autumn evening of 1863, after a long journey from Westmorland. He found St. John's Wood, but was then sent to Highgate Hill, whence he was returned at length to Kilburn Gate, and eventually reached his destination. After a warm welcome, he was handed a paper of questions "to be thought and prayed over, and the answers returned" to the Principal. He was examined by the Rev. C. D. Marston, Rector of Bryanston Square, who asked what he thought and understood of the 17th Article?

"My hopes fell to zero, yet I replied at once that I had often read and thought about it, yet I was obliged to tell him that I did not understand so deep a truth. He did not dismiss me but said, 'I will write a satisfactory letter to the Principal.' I returned home, took the questions given me on paper, and returned them to St. John's Hall."

In due course he received a letter, dated September 17th, 1863, saying that his answers were satisfactory, and asking when it would be convenient for him to commence residence. He was the first student accepted, though the second in fact to reside, for Boultbee, anxious to get on with the good work, asked Francis Browne, a lieutenant in the Merchant Service, to come and read with him, in November, 1863, as already stated.

Lewthwaite arrived on January 20th, 1864. Prayers were said at 9.30 p.m., with a short discourse from Boultbee to the five students present on Gal. i. The next morning they again assembled for prayers at 10 a.m., and heard an address from the Principal on Gal. iv 7ff., discoursing on the work of the ministry, its requirements, trials, encouragements, and rewards. He particularly stressed the great need of preparation; if intelligence, powers of mind, and even so-called religion, were used for overthrowing the Word of God, how necessary it was that those preparing to become ministers of Christ should be first, men of God, and then of knowledge. One student at least never forgot this first address, and the prayer which followed, that all their endeavours, now begun, might be owned and blessed of God.

It was quickly becoming clear that enlarged premises must be procured. By November, 1865, Boultbee was asking the Council what upper limit they proposed to place on numbers admitted; what expenditure should be envisaged; and what policy should be followed as to selection. Yet in his view, the whole success of the College turned on this last point. It was in this that St. Bees, the non-graduate college founded in 1816, had failed; there, as he put it—

"the fatal idea ran through the whole transaction that men (if not immoral) were to be pressed through the Bishop's Examination, if the intellectual sieve would in any way permit the passage."

He found this question of selection a most difficult one, not least because he had become highly critical of the duly appointed clerical examiners, some of whom were not very discerning as to a candidate's character and suitability. He therefore suggested that examiners should be paid, and that the Rev. T. Green, Principal of the Church Missionary

College, Islington, with experience of this kind of work, should be included. This was agreed, and Mr. Green, together with the Rev. R. Gunnery, were accordingly appointed. It was also agreed that students should wear cap and gown, the pattern and choice being left to the Principal's discretion. A fortnight later, Boultbee was reporting to the Council on points which he had evidently been requested to ascertain, bearing in mind that the college would shortly be moving to new premises. The total cost for 1864 was £191 11s. 2d., and the average number boarded was 8·2. This gave an average cost for each student of £23 7s. 2d. The total cost for the first two terms of 1865 was £199 2s. 0d., and the average number boarded was 13·6, which would work out at £23 10s. 7d. for the full academic year of thirty-nine weeks. He estimated that teaching staff salaries for three tutors would be £1,000 per annum. Domestic staff was more difficult to calculate; but he would propose four maids at a total cost per annum of £51; and a man who would combine the offices of butler, waiter, and porter at £30 per annum, with board, lodging, and washing. A gardener would also be necessary for the larger premises in view; he might also clean knives and shoes at a suggested wage, if he lived out, of £1 a week. Extra service from charwomen might amount to £1 per month—an interesting commentary on the social and economic conditions of the times. Additional calculations for fuel, rates and insurance on the basis of twenty-four students would make for an average cost of £100 per student. An obvious problem was: Should all students pay the same fees? There followed an interesting comparison with three other theological colleges: at King's College, London, sixty students paid from £25 to £37 per annum for tuition only, eighty at St. Bees paid £21 for tuition only, and sixty to seventy at St. Aidan's paid £80 per annum all in. He therefore suggested £45 per annum as being reasonable fees for all. The points on which he requested immediate guidance were:

1. The scale of establishment to be sanctioned and the appointment of a second tutor.
2. The fees to be asked, whether of all alike, or of two separate classes of students.
3. The case of University men—whether to live in College and what fees to be payable.
4. The case of students proposing to live with friends, or (being married) to live at home.
5. The number of students to be admitted the following January.

But within a few months a move had taken place. More commodious premises were obtained by the purchase of buildings at Highbury, with some seven acres of land. These had begun as a Congregationalist College in 1825, and when about 1850, New College was founded from the former Coward College, Homerton College, and Highbury College, the latter buildings were taken by the Metropolitan Training Institution for Schoolmasters. This had recently come to an end, and provided a suitable location for the new Anglican foundation. It was to be the College's home until the bombing of World War II obliged evacuation to another locality in 1942.

Looking back six months, Boultbee could record in June, 1866, his gratitude that builder and architect had kept faith to the day. To move into his new house on January 23rd and to receive the students on the 24th involved considerable organisation, but the work was resumed without interruption. Already a feeling of pride in their new surroundings was notable among the men. One immediate problem was that of fees. Boultbee was doubtful whether a steady supply of men could be found to pay £70 per annum for three years, when a man of fair ability could, by the aid of scholarships, graduate from Cambridge (and possibly Oxford) for about that sum, with the obvious advantage of a degree; yet at £35 per annum, the College could not be maintained, let alone developed. So far he had failed to find a third tutor, and would rather do without than have someone not up to standard.

With regard to relationships with King's College, the Principal, Dr. Jelf, had proposed two yearly examinations, a yearly fee of 5 guineas, and a final certificate signed by himself and the examiners. Boultbee, on the other hand, pointed out that six examinations were too many; he suggested instead three examinations, wholly exempting first-year men, and placing their tests at their second midsummer, their second Christmas, and at the end of their third year. Two examinations only might be better still, at the end of the second and third years, and 2 guineas a fairer fee than 5. As to the building, the east wing required refitting like the west, but the land required thorough draining, and improved fencing against petty trespass "on the part of a large and low population in the vicinity." A cheaper method of heating the library by hot water instead of the existing unsightly and expensive stove was also desirable, while additional shelves were needed. The Archbishop of York (Thomson), and the Bishops of Carlisle (Waldegrave), Ripon (Bickersteth), Peterborough

(Jeune), and Gloucester (Ellicott) would now receive Highbury men, and, he believed, also the Archbishop of Canterbury (Longley) and the Bishop of Winchester (C. R. Sumner). Finally, he had the immense satisfaction to record the first ordination, that of Lewis Sanders by the Bishop of Carlisle on Trinity Sunday, 1866, to the curacy of Wythop, Cockermouth, Cumberland. He was pleased to record that he had passed first in the examination, and had been specially commended. The Bishop reported that he was first in all subjects, "his work being sound, accurate and thoughtful, and his Hebrew good. This last particular gratified me," Boultbee continued, "as we cannot pretend in the time to bestow very much attention on that language; still, we aim at accuracy as far as we go." This first ordination was viewed with keen anticipation by the other students. Some of them rose earlier than usual to see him off on his long journey north, and it was recalled that "the fun-loving Henry Martin (who used to put books under his pillow with the pious wish that some of their learning would mysteriously distil into his brain during the night) jumped out of bed, threw his white counterpane round his shoulders like a Roman toga, and, in square College cap, he stood at the top of the stairs to give Sanders his valedictory benediction!" Great was the rejoicing when news arrived that he had been appointed gospeller at the ordination service in view of his first place in the examination, for much prayer had gone forth for him, and his success was taken as a mark of confidence in the College as a whole.

The first summer term in the new building was marked by a special gathering in the Principal's large drawing-room on June 5th, 1866, at which most of the Council members were present, including the Earl of Shaftesbury, the Hon. Arthur Kinnaird, M.P., the Revs. Alfred Peache, Daniel Wilson of Islington, Thomas Green of the Church Missionary College, and Messrs. Baxter and Hare. This was for most of the students their first opportunity of seeing Mr. Peache, and his address made a considerable impression. Basing his talk on II Tim. ii, he noted some of the necessary qualifications of a good minister of Jesus Christ, including fortitude, fidelity, and enduring hardness. On preaching, he warned his hearers not to spend too much time protesting against errors, and in controversy, but rather that they should "rightly divide the word of truth." He concluded:

"May the teaching at this College ever be in accordance with the charge which the apostle Paul in this chapter delivers to Timothy; and may the men who go forth from this place for the work of the ministry be such as he here describes, 'sanctified and meet for the Master's use, and prepared unto every good work.' "

His words, and those of others, made a considerable impression, and despite abundance of exhortation from most of those present, the day was long remembered with satisfaction. The extensive grounds at Highbury enabled sporting fixtures to be arranged. A College Cricket Club was formed in April, 1866, and the first match played on June 27th against the Church Missionary College, who scored 47 and 70, to which Highbury replied with 54 and in their second innings knocked off the required runs to win by nine wickets. On November 7th, however, in the first "soccer" match, the tables were turned, the C.M. College winning 5-0! This contact with men intending to work in the mission field brought a wider horizon before the men of the new College, many of whom were in due course also to fulfil their ministry abroad.

In this year also an Elocution Society was formed, an offshoot of which was called "Sharp Practice"; this entailed writing a subject on slips of paper, placing them in an urn, each drawing one out and having to speak on that subject for five minutes. Debates were encouraged, and Shakespeare readings, and at length the Society came to hold weekly meetings throughout each term.

The first College magazine appeared in manuscript form in 1868 under the editorship of Joseph Last. It contained contributions from staff and students on such subjects as the Irish Church Question. Recollections of the Isle of Wight, the Huguenots, A Walk to Cambridge, and the Pan-Anglican Synod (i.e. the first Lambeth Conference, of 1867), and some poems by W. St. Hill Bourne, who later wrote "The Sower went forth sowing." It also included a College diary, giving news of College societies and sport. It records how, once again, "the Church Missionary men" in a football match that lasted two hours, playing with "considerable spirit on both sides" throughout, beat Highbury 4-0; and once again St. John's obtained revenge winning the cricket match by the comfortable margin of 45 runs. Contributions to the magazine, however, were not always sufficiently numerous, which drew forth an amusing editorial *cri de cœur* in 1873 in a parody of "The Walrus and the Carpenter."

"The Porpoise and the Editor had taken each a pen;
    They wept like anything to see such quantities of men;
    If they would only something write it would be grand, and then . . .

If many men with many a pen should write for half a year,
'Do you suppose,' the Porpoise said, '*one* number would appear?'
'I doubt it,' said the Editor, and shed a bitter tear."

The magazine remained in manuscript form until 1885, with at times most elaborate pen-and-ink illustrations; it was then succeeded by a printed issue, *St. John's Magazine*, which changed to *The Johnian* in 1907, and this name it still carries.

In January, 1869, the St. John's Hall Clerical Union was formed. At this time the number of ordained students was ten, and most of them came on to the reunion from the Islington Clerical Conference held the same day. Among the Reunion visitors were the Bishop of Huron (Cronin), Canon Burgess, and Messrs. Ditcher and A. M. W. Christopher. Among the rules drawn up were the fixing of an annual subscription of one shilling (this was increased at subsequent intervals!); that a committee should arrange subjects for discussion at an annual gathering to be held each January, not to exceed three hours in duration. The first paper was read by the Rev. T. Lewthwaite on January 18th, 1870, on "How can we, as ministers of the Word, best secure and retain that high degree of spiritual life which is alone consistent with our office, and at the same time, for the sake of souls, go in and out among men irreligious and immersed in the things of this world?" Other papers dealt with neglect of visiting, the problem of ministry in large cities, and how to maintain contact with children after leaving Sunday school—all highly practical subjects. The first committee of the union was elected with the Rev. George Herbert as President; Vice-Presidents: Revs. Thomas Lewthwaite and W. J. Noble; with Henry Lansdell as Honorary Secretary. Among later controversial rules was added one which stated that the Union should only consist of those members of the College who were in sympathy with the principles of the Church of England as laid down in the Trust Deed of the College. This caused considerable heart-burnings on a number of occasions, until its subsequent revision. Mrs. Boultbee in after years stated that it was she who had suggested to Mr. Peache that the January gathering should be an annual affair. The first organised effort was a clerical fund, primarily to provide prizes for students, with Lansdell as Secretary. In 1873, the first student, the Rev. J. F. Browne, became President, and the Rev. Joseph Last, Secretary. Subsequent Presidents have included such stalwarts as Thomas Lewthwaite, Henry Lansdell, Prebendary E. Grose Hodge, S. A. Johnston, W. Laporte Payne;

while among Secretaries, T. P. Stevens, H. Bloomer, S. A. Johnston, A. E. Worsley, F. Pring Rowe, the indefatigable R. F. Penfold, and the present secretary, the Rev. T. G. Jones, have all exhibited devotion to the College interests and maintained the Union as a lively body, always ready to keep members in touch with current College activities.

Boultbee was much in request as a speaker on the whole question of clerical training. At the Church congress at Nottingham of 1871 on the subject "Clerical Education in Connection with the Universities and Theological Colleges," where other speakers included Professor Westcott, Edward King, Principal of Cuddesdon College, and E. W. Benson, the future Archbishop, Boultbee stated that in 1870 some 412 graduates were ordained and 135 non-graduates—a ratio of about 4 to 1. He would like to see the course extended from two to three years, and he pointed out the advantage of a theological college in that men could be selected, whereas that was not possible in a university. Another speaker, however, expressed the hope that the majority of the clergy would always receive their training in the universities. Two years later, at a Church Congress at Bath, Boultbee stated that until a few years previously the universities of Oxford and Cambridge had almost a monopoly of the candidates for the ministry, but now that they could not supply the numbers needed, many ordinands must be sought elsewhere. The young men were available, and they could be educated in the theological colleges, but Boultbee put in a powerful plea that such colleges should be officially recognised, not (as in many cases) barely tolerated. He advocated a centrally controlled examination for men from such colleges, which would produce much better results.

To the great satisfaction of the College, the degree of Doctor of Laws was conferred on Boultbee by Cambridge University in 1871. In 1869, the Rev. William Jones, formerly Scholar of Emmanuel College, Cambridge, joined the staff for two years, and in 1871 the Rev. R. H. Rodgers, formerly Scholar of Brasenose College, Oxford, and Denyer and Johnson scholar, while the Rev. Gordon Calthrop, Vicar of St. Augustine's, Highbury New Park, was engaged to give lectures in sermon composition. By 1872 the College had found its feet, and at the annual meeting of Council, friends, and former students on January 17th, that year, the Principal made an important statement on the position and needs of the new foundation. Set out in tabular form, the position was as follows:

	Students in training	Ordained
1864	10	1
1865	14	1
1866	22	6
1867	27	5
1868	31	9
1869	43	13
1870	44	12
1871	40	17

Former students were now working in seventeen dioceses, and the college was becoming generally known, but it was regarded as a peculiarly "narrow" institution in its religious outlook. Evidently the Principal took this accusation to heart, for he spent a considerable part of his address in a vigorous refutation of the charge:

"The college had never shrunk from a distinct avowal of our principles. . . . I suppose that is what people nowadays call 'narrow.' It is a word which this age for some reason of its own has chosen to fasten peculiarly upon those whom the previous age nicknamed Evangelicals, and whom this age abuses for having accepted the name."

This aroused a passionate protest from Boultbee:

"You may be a Ritualist and drive out half your parishoners by your antics, and you won't be called 'narrow', though you posture within the smallest of circles. You may be a stiff High Churchman, and coolly deny to your Presbyterian brother any standing whatever. Yet you are not called narrow, though you are entrenched within the most unyielding bounds of the Apostolic Succession. You may be a Liberal of the Modern school, denying to the poor Churchman even so much as the use of God's Word in the school where his children are taught, though he, poor man, is narrow enough to think that no education on any other basis is worth having. No matter, he is narrow. You who deny it him are liberal. But if you are a Churchman, according to the definition of our trust deed, holding boldly and fully what you know to be the definite teaching of your own Church, and which you are also persuaded is firmly based on Holy Scripture, you are narrow. . . . All this is a strange paradox. . . . If I take on the one side the criticisms of the *Record*, the *Christian Observer*, the *Christian Advocate*, the *Rock*, and some others of the same school, I find that, if there be one thing for which they give me credit, it is fairness and candour, and I may add that I have noted the word 'fair' applied to my work in private letters from the leading divinity professors in the universities. I turn to the organs on the other side of the Church, and I select these expressions, 'very one-sided indeed,' a 'partisan book' "—

29

in reference to his recently published work on the Thirty-nine Articles. After quoting various unfavourable criticisms of his work from the *Methodist Recorder*, the *Atheneum*, and the *Literary Churchman*, he continued:

> "We say boldly that we stand by the faith of Cranmer, Ridley, Jewel, Parker, Whitgift, Hooker, Hall, Barrow, Tillotson, Pearson, and all the great representative men of the English Church. . . .We feel that we are true soldiers in the great host to which they belonged, and that their banner is ours, and so whether it be called narrow, or any other dimension of space, we do not greatly care."

This renewed declaration of the College's position, and of his own views was received with loud acclamation.

He felt obliged to return to the subject two years later in 1874, to answer the taunt that here was a group of men, shut up in a small college. He indignantly denied that this must involve isolation in thought or activity. After all, they were in London, not in some small provincial town, and so could hardly escape contact with the changes of the times. They were not like seminary priests, segregated at an early age, but rather like the young lawyer or doctor, "subjected to a temporary technical training, but not isolated for it." They came from many walks of life, from the Services and the professions, with a few Oxford and Cambridge graduates, and where better could preliminary clerical training and experience be gained than in London, which could provide opportunities of school-teaching, preaching, and sick-visiting? Such practical Christian work was of immense value. The matter of narrowness has been considered at some length, for it has been a charge constantly levelled against Evangelicals, not always without a suspicion of truth. In these circumstances, however, it would appear that Boultbee was more than able to hold his own in pointing to the positive nature of the training which he sought to give, which must ever remain the most attractive and powerful Evangelical contribution to the Anglican Church.

But he also drew attention to a pressing problem—the provision of suitable accommodation. The existing dining-hall was crowded and inconvenient and the lecture-rooms small and ill-ventilated, which would be immediately condemned at any national school inspection.

> "We want a dining-hall and a chapel, on a scale of magnitude suitable to present purposes, and wisely calculated with a view to any possible contingencies of increase which may take place in future years. This would set

free portions of the present building, which would at once give us proper lecture rooms. Until this is done, further expansion is impossible."

He went on with suitable diffidence:

"I feel a delicacy about such allusions in the presence of our generous founder,"

but continued by expressing the hope that

"God might put it into someone's heart to give us these buildings. . . . If we see private individuals coming forward with such large gifts for the erection of the large and stately Keble College in Oxford, which is crowded with students under no dubious theological influence, is it too much to hope that some enlightened Protestant Christians may be found ready to supplement our deficiencies, and to fill up our comparatively humble and modest requirements? There can be no question that a very large part of our troubles in the Church of England has arisen from the almost utter neglect of educational institutions by our side of the Church. They have been allowed to drift into the hands of others, and until we awake to the importance of this matter, and take measures for being more accurately and sufficiently represented educationally, how can we fairly complain of the stream when we neglect the fountain?"

The suggestion as to the new dining-hall was immediately approved, and building operations began without delay. It was completed in 1875, a large part of the cost being defrayed by the founder and his sister. In his speech on June 26th at a gathering to celebrate the opening of the new hall and other College buildings, the Principal set out his views on the purpose and work of the College. The concern of the Council had not been for the mere increase of clergy, but to train and send forth men for the strengthening of the Church's spiritual life and witness. Some said such men were not to be found; but they had been found; some fifty-five of them were then in residence, and over 130 were scattered throughout the parishes of England or working abroad. Turning to the academic side, he stated that men from non-graduate theological colleges were now examined side by side with university men, and it had been proved in these examinations that men from St. John's Hall were able to hold their own and take a good place in the class lists thrown open to them. In time this would vindicate their position, and give them the confidence of their fellow Churchmen. He was glad to acknowledge many examples of kindness from the bishops, from examining chaplains, and especially from Dr. Westcott, Regius Professor of Divinity at Cambridge, "who had been pleased to speak most encouragingly after his personal examination of the candidates from this college in the [recently instituted] General Examination."

This only served to emphasise what he had said at the reunion. He had then recognised that the weak point of non-graduate colleges was their lack of recognition by those in authority. However able or well-read a student might be, he had no public means of proving it. It was an admitted disadvantage to the student and to the Church, which was entitled to some public assurance that her ministers were sufficiently educated. The great difficulty had been the lack of a general public examination to which all might be admitted. Now to his satisfaction such an examination had been inaugurated, and Highbury men had achieved great credit; out of thirteen candidates who sat for the examination, five had got a first-class, and eight a second. "I rejoice to see those class lists," he exclaimed, "and to observe the names of our own students coming out side by side with those of university men, of fellows of colleges, and of members of similar institutions throughout the country." He went on to pay tribute to Professors Westcott and Lightfoot, and to make a significant suggestion: that the one thing wanting was some authorised honorary designation to be used by those who pass the examinations. Exactly sixty years later, so far as the Highbury examinations were concerned, his wish was fulfilled in the granting of the associateship of the London College of Divinity.

At the annual meeting of January 19th, 1876, Dr. Boultbee was presented by Mr. Lewthwaite, on behalf of all Johnians, past and present, with a testimonial consisting of a silver epergne and articles of carved oak study furniture, for which £175 had been subscribed. At the College breakfast the following morning Mrs. Waller presented Mrs. Boultbee with a cheque for £50 for a piano.

It was then reported that 142 students had been ordained from the College, while its numbers were the highest on record, at fifty-seven. The first missionary from the College had just sailed, the Rev. James Stone, being appointed by C.M.S. to the Telugu Mission. Boultbee also noted that the Rev. D. M. Berry, late Demy of Magdalen College, Oxford, and Ellerton Prizeman, had become Resident Tutor, succeeding the Rev. R. H. Rodgers, who had resigned from ill-health. Mr. Peache's remarks on this occasion drew attention to the need for remaining faithful to the principles on which the College was founded, warning the members present that if anyone did not "preach and teach distinctively Protestant and evangelical doctrines, they are no true members of our Society." At a subsequent meeting, he likened himself and Boultbee to two partners in a firm: "he supplies the brains, and I supply the brass"!

College numbers continued to increase: sixty-five were in residence in 1878, and by the following year almost two-hundred had been ordained. Yet the Hall was not paying its way, and was being subsidised by Peache to the tune of £400 per annum. The Council therefore agreed to raise the fees to £70 per annum. An important matter of policy was now raised. A former student had completely changed his views, and after examination of the case, the Principal had authorised the removal of his name from the College Calendar. The man was demanding his reinstatement. The Council argued that the Calendar was a purely voluntary publication, but in case of difficulty it was determined to take Counsel's opinion. Counsel upheld Boultbee's action, but the incident served to show, in the opinion of many, the need to give heed to Peache's warning to remain true to those principles for which the College was founded.

Former students had raised over £4,000 towards the completion of the College buildings, and the Council received the gift with warm appreciation. Once again accommodation was becoming inadequate (in 1880 numbers had for a short time reached seventy-five), and some had been heard to say that the College was becoming too large, making additional staff necessary. Accordingly, the Rev. Henry Gee was appointed Tutor. Former Symes Scholar of Exeter College, Oxford, he had taken a second class in Moderations, and a third Class in Theology, with Junior Hall Houghton and Denyer and Johnson Prizes, and for twenty years he rendered outstanding service to the College before being appointed Principal of Bishop's College, Ripon, from 1900 to 1902: and Master of University College, Durham, from 1902 to 1918; B.D. and D.D. Oxon, 1898, he was Dean of Gloucester from 1917 to 1938. He is best remembered for his joint authorship, with W. J. Hardy, of *Documents Illustrative of English Church History*, which first appeared in 1896.

Once again criticism had been directed at the College, to which the Principal saw fit to reply at the annual gathering of January, 1881. It was a criticism to which he appears to have been peculiarly sensitive— that the College too closely resembled a Roman Catholic seminary, and that it was too conservative in outlook. He denied that they were "shut up within narrow lines of thought, frowzy and ill-ventilated. But we have matured convictions. We stand upon our right to teach heartily, really and truly the old Protestant doctrine. . . . Why," he asked, "may we not choose and maintain the good old Protestant School which we believe most clearly represents the revealed doctrine of the Word of God? This we avow: this we hope to hand down to our successors." If this further reference to narrowness of views should arouse suspicion that "there is no smoke without a fire," it should be borne in mind that this was a period of considerable advance in the methods of clerical training. Evangelicals had grasped the importance of this principle, and were busy on a number of new projects. As a result of two articles appearing in the *Christian Observer* in July and August, by E. H. Carr, entitled "The Establishment of an Institution for the Theological Preparation of the Clergy—an Appeal" and "The Professional Instruction of the Clergy," moves were set on foot which led to the foundation of Wycliffe Hall, Oxford, in 1877, and Ridley Hall, Cambridge in 1879, though it did not open until 1881. The Keswick Convention was first held in 1875, while the founding of the Scripture Union, Childrens' Special Service Mission and Cambridge Inter-Collegiate Christian Union all belong to this period. Such activities were bound to draw attention to Evangelical beliefs and practice, with corresponding criticisms of alleged shortcomings; in this setting, therefore, Boultbee's attention to adverse criticism does not appear excessive.

The year 1881 saw the inauguration of a new staff appointment. In July 1880, Mrs. Whitehead, of Amberley Court, Gloucestershire, had written proposing to found a professorship of preaching and of pastoral theology in memory of her husband, Ralph R. Whitehead, Esq. The Council had accepted the offer with sincere thanks: it involved a gift of £1,310, and Canon James Fleming, B.D., who had been lecturing on elocution and reading in the College since 1873, became the first holder of the chair from 1881 to 1887. Soon afterwards came the endowment of another professorship. Chiefly through the influence of Dean Close of Carlisle, £5,000 was subscribed to perpetuate the memory of the former Dean of Ripon, Dr. Hugh McNeile, who had exercised an outstanding ministry for over fifty years. The trust deed stated that the professor should—

> "give such instruction as shall best prepare the students for the duty of preaching and expounding to the people the true meaning and application of Holy Scripture as it is set forth in the original tongues, wherein 'holy men of God spake as they were moved by the Holy Ghost,' and in all his teaching [the professor] shall so order himself as may best serve, in accordance

with the Thirty-nine Articles of the Church of England, to the salvation of souls and the glory of God."

The first appointment was entrusted to the tutor, the Rev. Charles Waller, D.D., who held it from 1882 to 1898. The year 1881 also saw the first association of another significant figure with the College, for the Rev. William Hagger Barlow now became examiner for admission of candidates, in place of the Rev. R. Gunnery, of St. Mary's, Hornsey Rise. Dr. Barlow, then Principal of the Church Missionary College, Islington, became a Prebendary of St. Paul's from 1898 to 1901, and President of the College Council and Dean of Peterborough until his death in 1908. The Rev. F. E. Wigam was appointed to the College Council in 1882.

This year also brought an important building development:

> "If we are no longer young," remarked the Principal at the annual gathering, "it seems time that any remaining deficiencies in our building should be supplied. I have often recapitulated these. Lecture rooms, Chapel, infirmary, tutors' rooms and gateway lodges were the chief items for which our appeal went forth. The amount received so far has been £7,200, and something more is promised."

His words were once again listened to by Alfred Peache, and within two months he and his sister had offered £5,200 for the building of the chapel. The work on this and other buildings, under the architect, Evan Christian, made steady progress, and was completed within two years. The front gateway was designed to resemble that of St. John's, Cambridge, Dr. Boultbee's old College.

On St. Luke's Day, 1882, Dr. Boultbee preached what Handley Moule called "a noble sermon", at the opening and dedication of the additional buildings at Ridley Hall, Cambridge.[1] His subject was the fate of the disobedient prophet, and was, in the opinion of another present, "full of power and suggestion."[2] It was an intense pleasure to the Principal that, exactly twenty years after he first came to study at Kilburn, the first student, J. F. Browne, was made Archdeacon of Madras, and the B.D. degree conferred upon him by Archbishop Benson. Also in 1883, Bishop Jackson of London gave well-deserved recognition to Boultbee's work at Highbury by appointing him Prebendary of Ealdland in St. Paul's Cathedral. In doing so, the Bishop spoke of the value of the College, which appreciation he believed was shared by the diocesan bishops generally.

[1] F. W. B. Bullock, *Ridley Hall*, vol. i, p. 353.
[2] *Record*, February 8th, 1884.

Unfortunately, Dr. Boultbee did not long enjoy this honour. For some time he had suffered from attacks of gout, and had had to husband his strength. He went for a holiday to Bournemouth and died suddenly on January 30th, 1884, aged sixty-five years. His burial took place on February 6th at Chesham, Bucks, where his second son, Charles, was Vicar. The Rev. Gordon Calthrop conducted the service. Among the congregation, in addition to relatives and college staff, were a large number of Dr. Boultbee's former students. Two days later,[1] Bishop Ryle of Liverpool preached a memorial sermon at Christchurch, Highbury, on John xi. 11. He spoke of the heavy loss sustained by the college and by the whole Church of England. Dr. Boultbee was "a well-balanced, well-proportioned theologian, drawing all his creed from the Scriptures, of a holy and consistent life," and always about his Master's business. There were very few of whom he had heard so little criticism spoken as of Dr. Boultbee. He was—

> "true as steel to the grand leading verities of the Reformation, but able at the same time to make allowance for differences of opinion, and never forgetting that in a fallen world men will not always interpret language in the same way."

Dr. Boultbee's book on the Articles was the best on the subject that had ever been published. It had only one fault—it was too short. The Bishop stated that while he had consulted many men during his ministry, Dr. Boultbee had a peculiar wisdom which made his counsel invaluable. He was also an admirable Principal. He had begun with many predictions of failure from his enemies and fears among his friends, but he had worked on patiently and quietly with annually growing success. The Bishop concluded: "Let us pray for Highbury that . . . the light kindled there may never burn dim, and never be extinguished." Many tributes were paid to Dr. Boultbee: including one from an old student who referred to the quiet dignity and reserve which prevented the taking of liberties, but never repelled. If a rebuke was necessary, it was given in a few pointed and grave words, "with a father's affection and full of courtesy," while his whole life inspired both respect and love, springing from the knowledge that the Principal was a man of earnest prayer. The College Council expressed in their minutes their deep grief on account of the Principal's death, stating "that it will be vain to seek for one to succeed him who has

[1] *Record*, February 8th, 1884.

all the peculiar excellencies which he possessed." They continued:

"It is a matter which calls for greatest thankfulness that for twenty years there has been such a man at the head of this Institution, and that no less than 300 clergymen have had the benefit of his training and instruction."

And the Council earnestly prayed that—

"the impress of his sound Scriptural teaching and beautiful Christian example may never be effaced from the College, but that all who succeed him may be followers of him as he was of his blessed Lord and Master."

In addition to his book on the Thirty-nine Articles, Dr. Boultbee had written in 1879 *A History of the Church of England—Pre-Reformation Period*, and several volumes of sermons. He gave the annual address at the Victoria Institute in 1873, and, as previously mentioned, read papers at various Church congresses on subjects connected with clergy training, while in 1881 he preached the C.M.S. anniversary sermon at St. Bride's, Fleet Street.

The measure of Boultbee's achievement must be the fact that in twenty years he had made the College known and respected by the bishops, who with increasing confidence, received his candidates for ordination. The reputation of a college rests heavily upon the character of its principal. Boultbee's faithful adherence to his convictions, careful teaching, and sympathetic oversight of more than 300 men during this period, brought to the ministry of the Church of England a strengthening of Evangelical witness, by sending out candidates who compared by no means unfavourably, both on the academic and spiritual levels, with those who, from a human standpoint, commenced their work with greater advantages.

CHAPTER II

Consolidation of influence, 1884-99

I T was not surprising, in view of his previous work and saintly
character, that Dr. Waller should be the unanimous choice of the
Council to succeed Dr. Boultbee as Principal. His early career had
been distinguished. Educated at Bromsgrove School, he gained a scholarship to University College, Oxford, where he took a first class in Moderations, a second class in Mathematical Moderations, and a second class
in Lit. Hum. He was ordained to the curacy of St. Jude's, Mildmay Park,
but the strain of a busy city parish was too much for his health, and,
on Mr. (later Canon) Christopher's recommendation he became tutor
at St. John's Hall. At first he also held a part-time curacy at Christ
Church, Mayfair, and afterwards the Readership of Curzon Chapel
under the future Bishop Thorold. In 1867, he gained the first Denyer
and Johnson Theological Scholarship, and from 1870 he was for five
years in charge of St. John's Episcopal Chapel, Hampstead, but the
double work at the College and amongst his congregation proved
too much for him, and he resigned that office in 1875. With his pale
complexion, deep brown eyes and auburn beard, so well remembered
by his students, Dr. Waller was thus called upon to enter a period of
yet greater responsibility in the training of men for the ministry.

Opportunity was taken to make certain rearrangements in the
management of the College, bringing the Principal into direct personal
relations with the General Council and the Executive Committee, and
allowing him to appoint his own secretary and to nominate all tutors
and lecturers, who must be approved by the Executive Committee of
the Council before appointment. Also six new members were added
to the Council: Lord Harrowby, Sir John Kennaway, Bart., M.P.,
the Revs. E. R. Bernard, Vicar of Selbourne, Hants, W. H. Barlow,
already mentioned, J. F. Kitto, Rector of Stepney, and W. Fuller, Esq.
Early in 1885, Bishop Frederick Temple of London, who had succeeded
Bishop Jackson that year, paid his first visit to the College. The future

Archbishop of Canterbury paid tribute to the work of the institution, and to its founder and first Principal. As a result, St. John's Hall was recognised as a diocesan college of the London Diocese and of the Province of Canterbury. The College hood, which was first granted in 1873, was changed at this time from black with maroon edging to black with a scarlet binding, which it still retains. In 1890, however, Archbishop Thomson of York disallowed its use on the ground that it was not a tippet; the Council therefore decided to alter the hood, in accordance with the Canon. The matter fell through, however, owing to the Archbishop's death, and was not raised again.

In the autumn of 1885 occurred the death of the College's first President, Lord Shaftesbury, and the Council recorded its sorrow, with a tribute to the great interest which he had shown in its foundation and development. The Earl of Harrowby, K.G., was elected in his place. The College continued to prosper under its new Principal. In 1885, the annual clerical reunion, which had been held in January to coincide with the Islington conference, was changed to the time of the May meeting of the missionary societies. An addition to the staff in 1885 was the appointment of the Rev. J. A. Lightfoot as tutor. He had taken a third class in Theology at Hertford College, Oxford, and remained until 1893. He was Principal of the C.M. College, Islington, from 1899 to 1917. Two years later, Canon Fleming having resigned as Whitehead Professor, the Rev. Gordon Calthrop, Vicar of St. Augustine's, Highbury, and for many years connected with the College as lecturer, was appointed to succeed him. As Mr. Irving Hare was finding the office of Honorary Treasurer too great a burden, the new Lord Kinnaird, for long a Council member, agreed to assist him in this office.

A fund had been opened in memory of Dr. Boultbee, and this had grown by 1886 to £660. It was agreed that £100 should be expended on a portrait of the first Principal, painted by Wontner, which still hangs in the dining-hall; the remainder was presented as a token of affection and gratitude to Mrs. Boultbee.

In 1888 new arrangements were made for the celebration of Founder's Day. It was decided to make this into a three-day conference meeting at the College from May 1st to 4th. Papers were read by two old Johnians, the Revs. P. F. J. Pearce, Vicar of Pulloxhill, Bedfordshire, on the necessity for a robust Christian character, and G. E. Ford, Vicar of Holy Trinity, Bristol, on the need to follow the apostolic example to preach "Jesus and the Resurrection." The success of this gathering led to its adoption as the usual procedure until the War of 1914–18 put a stop to such meetings. A society which has exercised an important influence on the life of the College, the Vigiles Association, was founded in 1889, as a continuation of the Prayer Union; it is merely noted at this point, for its activities will receive further treatment in a subsequent chapter. The health of the students is sometimes referred to; usually it was good, but we find a note of three accidents, "two with a cricket ball, and one on the railway": fortunately none of them was serious.

The Founder's Day of 1891 was a particularly notable occasion, for nearly 130 former members of the College accepted invitations, and the Rev. Thomas Lewthwaite, Vicar of All Souls, Haley Hill, Halifax, was chosen to make a presentation to the Principal in recognition of his twenty-six years of service to the College. Just over 100 guineas had been subscribed, and from it the Principal received a silver cup and pedestal, together with a purse for the payment of fees for the B.D. and D.D. degrees of Oxford University, which were to be conferred upon him. In the evening, an address was given by the Rev. Dr. Wace, Principal of King's College, London, on the subject of "Inspiration." This was the first time that the Principal of King's had attended a re-union. A new teaching University for London was granted to the joint petitions of King's and University Colleges. "We hope," said Dr. Waller, "that the B.A. degree will by this means be brought within the reach of Highbury students . . . with the assistance of preparation by our own College tutors."

Life in College at this time flowed on at a fairly even pace without undue incident. A drop in the number of students to forty-three occurred in 1892, but it quickly grew to 67 by the end of the year, though it dropped to 44 in 1894. At this time the Principal requested the Council to advise him as to the desirability of supplying beer to the students each day, and to the College servants. A report on the matter was called for, and after consideration the Council decided that the practice should be continued, but that it should only be done at extra charge. The impression is gained that life was rather too easy-going, and that discipline left something to be desired. One student had completed his three-year course, and then had withdrawn from receiving Holy Orders—the first example of its kind. Changes in staff included the appointment in 1893 of the Rev. E. H. M. Waller, Scholar of Corpus Christi College, Cambridge, eldest son of the Principal, and in 1895 of the Rev. S. C. E. Legg, Scholar of Caius

College, Cambridge, Tyrwhitt Hebrew Scholar and Mason Prizeman, as tutors. Also in 1894, on the resignation of Prebendary Calthrop, the Rev. Edward Grose Hodge, Rector of Holy Trinity, Marylebone, a former Johnian, and past President of the Cambridge Union, was appointed Whitehead Professor. Of Prebendary Calthrop, one student, the Rev. Claud Wood, recalls:

"He had a large congregation at St. Augustine's and was a remarkable preacher. It was often difficult to get a seat. One member of his congregation was heard to say that he used to go to St. Mary's, Stoke Newington, because the music was so admirable, it was as good as going to a concert; but now he went to St. Augustine's, because the preacher was so dramatic it was as good as going to the theatre. His sermons were always written, and he declared that he could not preach without his manuscript, but one did not know he was reading."

Something of a crisis in the academic life of the College occurred in 1896, when a statement on its position was made by Dr. Peache. Its immediate cause was the establishment of the new preliminary classical examination required by bishops to be taken by non-graduate students before entering theological colleges. It was held by some to be responsible for the closures of St. Bees and Gloucester Colleges. He felt that many non-graduates would now be debarred from entering the Church of England by this new requirement, because sufficient time would not be allowed for the additional work, if this examination were taken instead of the first year's course. He wanted the bishops to know of the College's difficulty on this account, believing that if this were done, instead of the number of students declining, it would increase. The Council took the matter seriously, and ordered the following statement to be included in the College calendar:

"The full course for non-graduates at St. John's Hall being three years, it must not be assumed that this course can be reduced to two years by simply passing the Bishops' examination. There is no limit of age for nomination to sit for this examination. And manifestly the youth who could easily pass it at eighteen is not within two years of Holy Orders either in point of age or in point of preparation; while to a business man of twenty-five or six, who left school at fifteen, knowing little Latin and no Greek, the examination may be formidable. Again, to another man of the same age, well-trained in such practical work as laymen often do in our large parishes, scholastic requirements may seem superfluous. Yet they are indispensable to the clergymen who would take competent charge of a place where all classes of society may be found. Moreover the quiet preparation of the first year is invaluable,

41

not only for the Bishops' entrance examination, which would be advantage-
ously passed in the first two terms if possible; but for valuable instruction
in the elements of Bible study, and in the doctrine of the 39 Articles, which
are a subject in the course of the first year."

After reading this statement, intending students could be in no doubt
as to the College's feelings on this matter, even if for the time being they
were obliged to conform to the new requirements. Students entries
for the years 1893-6 inclusive had totalled ninety-four, an average intake
per year of only twenty-three. The Principal presented a memorandum
setting out the difficulties caused by the new academic requirements,
which contained the statement:

"It is inconvenient enough to have our course commencing twice in the
year; we cannot commence it at three different times. . . . The scramble for
examination in the first year often proves injurious to students through the
strain it puts upon them, the almost inevitable cramming of things that
ought not to be crammed: as the entire outline of sacred history for a paper
which any intelligent schoolboy from a national school might pass; and the
disturbance of quiet thoughtful study which might otherwise be continued
until the third year, without any examination except those which are held
in College, and on the lines of College teaching."

In the case of students who did not come until after they had passed
the entrance examination, the loss would be much more serious, for
they would only have a bare two years, having done no work on the
Bible, none on the Articles, and no Church history. He concluded by
saying: "To a student [entering directly from a classical school] the
examination does mischief; to a man of 25 or 26 it may be formidable,
but it interferes less with his proper training." He asked for guidance
on the following question: If seven terms were insisted upon after
passing the entrance examination, would this put the College at a
disadvantage with other colleges? Could they attempt a "preparatory"
department, with provision for evening classes? Or could they insist
on an examination in certain theological papers before men began their
final two years of study in the College? The sub-committee appointed
to consider the question largely endorsed the Principal's memorandum,
and recommended flexibility for a first year of one, two, or three
terms, but felt that the "quiet preparation" of the full year was invaluable when possible. There, for the moment, the matter was allowed to
rest. These internal difficulties were in the main obscured from general
knowledge, partly due to the rejoicing at the appointment of John

Taylor Smith as the College's first Bishop. On the resignation of Bishop Ingham, Taylor Smith, formerly Canon Missioner, was appointed Bishop of Sierra Leone in 1897. His fellow Johnians presented him with his episcopal robes at a special gathering on May 25th, in the presence of many friends, and of two African bishops, Oluwole and Phillips. His career will be considered later, but it can be stated here that few former members of the College were so beloved as he. Other movements affecting the College included the appointment of the Principal's eldest son Henry (E. H. M.) Waller to Allahabad in November 1897, under the Church Missionary Society, and his succession at Highbury by his brother, Cameron Waller, tutor in the Diocesan Training College, Montreal.

The reminiscences of a Johnian of this period give a picture of College life in the 1890's. Bishop Sherwood Jones (1895-7), formerly Suffragan Bishop of Hulme, has written:

> "The large ground adjoining the college, now the possession of the Arsenal Football Club, provided opportunity and encouragement for physical exercise, with its Fives courts, tennis court, football and cricket ground. The Cricket Eleven was exceptionally strong in these years: this was due in the main to the batting of F. H. Gillingham, who had recently come from Dulwich School, and who afterwards became so well known when he played for Essex and for the Gentlemen *v.* Players. Others in the team included Henry Waller as wicketkeeper, Douglas Gray and Sherwood Jones. On Sundays many of the men undertook voluntary service in north London parishes, including Spitalfields and Whitechapel, helping in the Sunday School, taking Open Air services and mission services. My experience took me to the Copenhagen Street Ragged School, where before one could begin a Bible lesson, one had to tell the latest news about cricket and other outside matters"—

including Mr. Gillingham's latest score! The Bishop goes on to record an experience while sitting at a harmonium during an open-air service, wearing the conventional frock coat, silk hat, and high "choker" collar. He was busily playing a hymn—

> "when a young nipper came behind me, squirted water down my neck, and was off like a flash! I could do nothing but grin and bear it! My high collar provided a temptation that he could not resist!"

Such experiences, and interruptions of a harsher kind, were by no means uncommon in open-air work, either then or in subsequent years.

The Rev. Claud Wood also recalls the appearance of the old football and cricket grounds, with—

"a pleasant walk round the edge under the shade of trees where we might converse with friends or read in the open air. The cricket pavilion backed on to the Principal's garden. Then came the cricket ground, on which quite good pitches could be obtained. A gardener kept it generally mown, but the players had to prepare the actual pitch. The captain often had trouble in prevailing upon players to help in rolling. Beyond the cricket ground was ample space for two football games. . . . All our cricket matches were played at home, so avoiding any expense of travel. Clubs were glad to come to a match with a club that had a ground to offer. . . . One year a chess tournament was organised and won by Muspratt, a Cambridge man who had played for the University and was doing a year at Highbury before ordination."

Such reminiscences from students give a picture of activities not thought worthy of normal record, though they remained a vivid memory in the minds of those who passed through the College at this time.

Changes had taken place in the College Council. In 1895 the then Suffragan Bishop of Coventry, E. A. Knox, was elected; and in 1898, on the death of the Rev. F. E. Wigram after fifteen years' service, Prebendary Wace was nominated to fill the vacancy. Both gave to the College long and devoted service.

The Principal's health was now giving much cause for concern. In 1898 the Council gave him leave of absence for six months, during which he went on a long sea voyage. The senior tutor, the Rev. Dr. Henry Gee was made acting Principal. As is well known, he was a man of very considerable ability who had been for some eighteen years at the College. He took a serious view of the situation, stating in his report that "the question not only of quantity, but also that of quality of students demands the careful consideration of the Council." Of the fifty students, twenty-one lived out of college, which meant that only twenty-nine paid full fees. In the Principal's absence, additional lectures were given by the Rev. W. H. Griffith Thomas, then Incumbent of Portman Chapel. The Rev. H. W. C. Geldart, Scholar of Emmanuel College, Cambridge, with a second class in the Classical Tripos, and later to become Principal of Bishop Wilson Theological College, was appointed resident tutor this year. Owing to the continuing decline in the College's fortunes, Dr. Barlow was sent by the Council to confer with the Archbishop of Canterbury in May, 1898, on the question of the entrance examination. On his return, he reported in July that Dr. Temple, who had visited the College and spoken to the students a few weeks before, had stressed the importance of the study of the Greek New Testament. He felt that he could not relax the standard of the examination in either Latin or Greek, but he might see his way to recommending alterations in the syllabus, especially in the matter of alternative books. The whole question would be discussed at a bishops' meeting in the new year. Gee's further statements continued gloomy, and increased the impression that nothing short of drastic changes would restore confidence in the future of the College. No first-classes had been gained in the University Preliminary Examination for the first time since 1882, and four out of ten candidates had failed the central examination, while three had been rejected by the Bishop of London at his own examination the month before (i.e. June). Gee had consulted with the Bishops of London and Durham, who had recommended not admitting men of more than thirty years old, and had insisted that all should take the full three-year course. The number of resident students was only thirty; in addition, twelve lived out. There had been complaints about the food, but these had now died down—altogether a dismal picture, for which there could be only one most regrettable remedy.

On his return from his six months' sick leave, Dr. Waller again reported that he felt considerable (if not unsuperable) difficulty would be experienced in satisfying the bishops' examination requirements. Thereupon the Council decided to take measures to secure the Principal's retirement. A careful letter was accordingly written pointing out that since the bishops required a two-year course after the central entrance examination, the Principal could hardly adapt his teaching and general procedure to the new system; he might therefore care to be relieved of his offices of Principal and McNeile Professor. This letter hurt Dr. Waller very deeply, as his reply makes clear. He stated that he would resign as Principal, but asked whether he could continue to hold the McNeile Professorship. This, however, the Council refused to allow, and at length Waller agreed, though he pointed out that his son Cameron would not have returned from Canada two years earlier had he suspected that his father would shortly retire. He offered his resignation at the close of the Lent Term, 1899, and accepted the pension which was offered him by the Council. Thus a painful period of indecision was brought to an end.

The Council was also faced with further difficulties. The condition of the College buildings was giving cause for anxiety. A firm of contractors had sent in an estimate for £1,600 for cleaning and re-decorating the Principal's house, making structural repairs to floors and walls, buttresses and fences, while recommending that an annual sum of at least £450 should be set aside as the minimum expenditure for maintenance.

The chief matter before them, however, was the choice of a new Principal. Among those approached were the Rev. F. J. Chavasse, Principal of Wycliffe Hall, and the Rev. T. W. Drury, Principal of the C.M. College, Islington. It was reported that Mr. Chavasse did not wish to leave Oxford, and the offer was made to Mr. Drury at a guaranteed salary of £700 per annum, with allowances for coal, gas, and internal repairs to the Principal's house. Another who was interviewed was the Rev. A. W. Greenup, Rector of Alburgh, Norfolk. The way in which he came to be considered is interesting. Greenup was walking along a Cambridge street when he was hailed by the then Dean of Westminster, Bishop H. E. Ryle. "Greenup," he said, "the Principalship of the London College of Divinity is vacant, and you are the right man for it. You must put in your application for it." This Greenup declined to do. "Very well," was the reply, "if you will not, I will place your name before the Council." This he did, which led to Greenup's appearance at the Council meeting, and to his being given full information on all matters concerning the College. However, Mr. Drury's appointment was agreed to by all seven of the Council members present at the meeting on February 23rd, 1899. Meanwhile, the Council were clearly determined that the appointment of all professors, tutors, and lecturers should not be vested in the Principal (as laid down in the original Trust Deed at the College's foundation), but should rest in their hands. They accordingly obtained permission from Dr. and Miss Peache to alter the deed so that staff appointments should be made in consultation with the Principal, but that final selection should be left to the Council. This was not only because of recent past experience; they added in the following important minute that it was because it would be—

> "a great help to the status of St. John's Hall if it could be recognised as part of the proposed new London University in which teaching colleges will be federated and their students entitled to offer themselves for degrees. It would strengthen the position of St. John's Hall in the country if this privilege could be obtained: but in order to secure it, it must be shown that the teaching staff is *adequate*, and to this end, it is desirable to show that such teaching staff is selected by the Council or governing body of the College."

It was also proposed that the appointment to the McNeile Professorship should be vested in the Council.

At a Council meeting of March 10th, however, Mr. Drury, who was present, declined the Principalship, and one can only presume that the reason why he should have left his decision so late was because he had also been offered the Principalship of Ridley Hall, Cambridge, which he accepted. A new short list was therefore drawn up, consisting of Dr. Gee, the senior tutor, and Messrs. Greenup and Griffith Thomas. After further enquiries, it was proposed and carried unanimously that the Rev. A. W. Greenup should be appointed Principal. He accepted, and his appointment was duly confirmed. Albert William Greenup was educated at the Leys School, Cambridge, and went up to St. John's as a foundation scholar. While there he held exhibitions in Hebrew and ecclesiastical history, and was Naden Divinity Student. Among his prizes were the University Prize in Hebrew, the Jeremie Septuagint and Tyrwhitt. In 1890 he took a first class in the Theological Tripos, being ordained the same year to a curacy at St. Matthew's, Cambridge. In 1893 he was appointed Chaplain to Earl Cadogan, Lord Lieutenant of Ireland from 1895 to 1902. Greenup was inducted to Alburgh in 1897. Meanwhile, Dr. Waller had presented his last report, which consisted of a dark picture of the College's position. It carried the warning note:

"If an unknown man is appointed [Principal] who will break the traditions of the College, it is not likely that he will draw students."

He continued with the flat statement that the new policy of having only two years to prepare for Orders made it impossible for non-graduate students to complete the work.

"The thing cannot be done. If [others] must needs throw away the lessons of more than thirty years in order to buy their own experience, that is their affair. My work is done, my testimony is given. I can only leave the matters in other hands."

It is difficult not to feel great sympathy for Dr. Waller, while also recognising that clearly the tasks involved in Principalship were now rather beyond his capacity. On leaving he was presented with an illuminated address and a cheque for £240. He went to live at Little Coxwell, Berkshire, until his death on May 9th, 1910.

He was a Principal much beloved by his students. An old friend recorded that:

"His ideal of fitness for the ministry was piety first, a sound knowledge of pastoral divinity next; and then classical ability. He regretted a tendency to reverse that order to the great detriment of the Church. . . . He always maintained that a way should be open into the ministry for godly men who had proved their ability by useful practical work."

He believed that most people cared little—

"for the niceties of speculative theology, that they need better fare than the critic's gospel can supply to help them in the trials and temptations of life."

He was a man of an intensely sympathetic nature; he could not tolerate insincerity and pretence, but to those in trial or difficulty he revealed the warmth of his love and support. Such a man was bound to place his standards of satisfaction higher than the mere passing of examinations. His own character radiated gentle humility and thoughtfulness for others, while his profound scholarship led him to deplore superficial work. Over 700 men passed into the ministry during his long connection with St. John's Hall, and to many of those he was a wise counsellor when they came to him with difficulties in their parochial ministries. He was a forthright advocate of the inspiration of the Bible, and strongly opposed the destructive work of the so-called "higher criticism." In his undergraduate days he had been deeply influenced by Dean Burgon, who, as Waller said, "made me what I am." Dr. Pusey had once said of Waller that he knew the Greek text of the New Testament better than most clergymen knew the English— a high tribute indeed from such a source.

His published works included *Grammar of the Words in the Greek Testament*, 1877, and *Analytical Vocabulary of Greek Testament Words*, 1878; and the following devotional commentaries, *Notes on the Prophet Jeremiah*, 1897; *Hosea, Joel and Amos*, 1904; also *When ye pray*, 1885; and an edition of Dean Burgon's *Seven Sermons on Inspiration and Interpretation*. He was examining chaplain to the Bishop of Liverpool from 1880 to 1899. He was not a great preacher; indeed, on one occasion he was seen to take out a stump of a pencil and alter his manuscript while the congregation patiently waited! But his obvious sincerity always commanded attention. His death provoked a moving tribute in verse from Bishop Handley Moule of Durham, with whom he had much in common, while a notable appreciation of his work was given in the memorial sermon preached in the College chapel by one of his former pupils, the Rev. Henry Pitt, Vicar of St. Mary's, Southwark, on May 12th, who said:

"He lived in close, intimate, personal communion with our Risen Lord. That was the power of his wonderfully active, self-denying life; that was the source of his cheerfulness in trial, his patience in labour, his wisdom in perplexity, his humility in the presence of his brethren. . . . I have seen him suffering from bodily weakness, yet patiently explaining at great length in writing the Scripture difficulties of a non-Conformist minister who by letter had applied to him, and at other times filling laborious hours in the preparation of notes for Sunday school teachers." And he concluded: "The chief desire of his heart, the main object of his life to which he consecrated all his great talents, was that he might serve the Lord faithfully, witnessing for Him in the midst of a crooked and perverse generation in sincerity and truth."

CHAPTER III

Ebb and Flow, 1899-1926

UPON the death of the Earl of Harrowby in March, 1900, the Council appointed the Rev. Alfred Peache, the founder of the College, as its next President. No more deserved or popular choice could have been made. Unfortunately, his tenure of office was all too brief, for he died in November of that year. The Council paid eloquent testimony to all that Dr. Peache had done; indeed, it was hard to find words which might suitably express all that the College owed to him. In financial benefactions alone, it was estimated that he and his sister from first to last gave some £120,000 towards the cost of the buildings, including the dining-hall, the chapel and the library, and for other needs. But his interest in Highbury men lasted far beyond their College course. Many references were made to his visits to parishes where Johnians were incumbents; to his wise advice when they confided in him their difficulties; and to the "fiver" tucked into a man's hand "to do what he liked with." He also founded the patronage trust which still bears his name. At the time of his death this numbered twenty-three livings, including Mangotsfield and Downend, of which he had been incumbent and where he was buried on November 27th, Dr. Waller giving the address. An old student recorded that—

> "in many an obscure rural parsonage, the incumbent and his wife . . . love to recall the days when the simple-hearted, unassuming, courteous old gentleman shared their somewhat frugal fare, [while their children] still remember the bright-faced old man, who had all their names and their birthdays down in the wonderful book he always carried about with him, and who made them feel that somehow they belonged to him, just as father did, because he was 'a Highbury man.'"

Peache loved to visit the squalid quarters, the drab back streets of the crowded city; to ask whether the young curate was keeping the Fourth Commandment and taking his day off regularly. When one old

50

Johnian was building a new church (Christ Church, Gorsley) and showed Dr. Peache the steadily rising walls, that good man asked: "What shall I give you for your church?" The incumbent replied that he would like a Communion table, which Peache promptly gave. Another aspect of his life-work should be mentioned—his association with Huron Theological College in Canada. Bishop Hellmuth enlisted his interest in this college, which was also founded in 1863; and Peache with further generosity offered to endow a divinity professorship there at a cost of some £5,000. Subsequently, when a charter was secured in 1878 for the Western University of Canada, situated at London, Ontario, Peache became its first Chancellor, and the degree of D.D. *honoris causa* was conferred upon him. He repeatedly wrote letters to former students warning them of the dangers of sacerdotalism and urging them "to hold together and encourage one another in bearing the reproach of the Cross." One such letter has been preserved, and on the envelope is written: "Please keep and read from time to time in memory when we are gone of the heartfelt sentiments of the founders of St. John's Hall, Highbury."

Few men have exhibited more clearly the character of a Christian steward; and though he had received much, he was a true successor of those early Evangelicals of the Clapham sect, devoting himself and his possessions to forwarding the Kingdom of God by every means in his power. His portrait, and that of his sister, bear an honoured place in the present College dining-hall.

A number of changes took place on the College Council at this period, those elected being in 1898 Prebendary Wace, and in 1899 Colonel the Hon. E. Legge, M.P., and the Rev. E. A. Stuart, Vicar of St. Matthew's, Bayswater, Professor H. C. G. Moule (later bishop of Durham), Canon Girdlestone, formerly Principal of Wycliffe Hall, Oxford, and Mr. J. F. W. Deacon; while Mr. James Round, M.P., was elected in 1900.

The new Principal's first task was to restore confidence in the financial and academic status of the College. His opening report outlined certain measures of retrenchment. Fuel could be saved by the closing of the west wing; staff salaries should be cut, and students charged for laundry. Some progress had been made in negotiations with London University for recognition of the College and staff. When Greenup himself applied for recognition as a university teacher, the Bishop of London (Mandell Creighton), one of the University Commissioners, wrote in reply: "Mr. Greenup has a list of subjects to his name which would put Solomon to shame"! It was decided that, since there were only twenty-five students, the services of the junior tutor (S. C. E. Legge) should be dispensed with. By the end of 1899, numbers had risen to thirty-four.

A serious view was taken by Dr. Gee in a report on the state of the library. For all practical purposes he termed it useless, containing too few modern books, with many incomplete sets, and many editions in bad condition. He requested a grant for the purchase of new books, and also that the College Secretary might be retained for a further period, on the ground that "those who really know the ins and outs of the College—the drains and hot-water pipes are a study in themselves—must realise the necessity of having someone who shall devote a great part of his time to bursarial duties." Greenup, on the other hand, advocated a tutor-bursar, and it is not difficult, in view of what followed, to detect a lack of sympathy between the comparative attitudes of Gee and Greenup on several important issues. Greenup also reported that he had started a Sunday evening Greek Testament reading in his drawing-room, followed by discussions, in order to provide informal opportunities for getting to know the men as soon as possible. As to practical work, he was unhappy about the position; each man was a law to himself. Some men went to Spitalfields, and the long walk there and back and the exacting nature of the work "made them incapable of close attention to lecture work on Monday"! He suggested that instead they should take up specific work nearer home, approved by him, such as in the new mission of Christ Church, Highbury, whose Vicar would welcome this help.

Within a few months, Dr. Gee sent in his resignation. After being associated with the work of the college for twenty years, he could not agree with the new policies being advocated. He felt that the whole objective of the College was being changed: "we are no longer in any sufficient sense of the words," he wrote, "a training College for Holy Orders, but are rather an establishment for preparing men to pass Bishops' Examinations." His resignation was accepted, and on leaving he was presented with an address and bookcase, with a cheque for £124, while a silver bowl was presented to Mrs. Gee. Gee was of a shy and reserved nature, but once students penetrated behind this reserve they found one who had their deepest interests much at heart. One student termed his lectures "by far the most helpful, directly useful and really inspiring that I attended at College." For some years he and his wife had presided over the hostel, and it was a coveted honour to be asked to tea there. Gee himself was not a good conversationalist, but Mrs. Gee soon put men at their ease, and became the confidante of many. For years afterwards Dr. and Mrs. Gee maintained their interest in Highbury men, often welcoming them as guests at University College, Durham, of which Gee became Master in 1902, after two years spent as Principal of Bishop's College, Ripon. Another who left the college in 1900 was the Rev. Cameron Waller. In 1902 he became Principal of Huron College, so strengthening the links between Huron and Highbury which had first been forged through Dr. Peache. In his place was appointed the Rev. E. H. Cox, formerly Scholar of Christ Church, Oxford, with a second class in Moderations and a second class in Lit. Hum. He had been curate of All Souls, Marylebone, since 1898. In place of Dr. Gee, the Rev. A. R. Whately was appointed Vice-Principal; formerly Scholar of Corpus Christi College, Cambridge, he took a second class in both parts of the Classical Tripos, and had been curate of St. John's, Wimborne, and of Kidbrook, Kent.

At the close of 1900, Greenup reported a slight decrease in numbers, thirty-six as against thirty-nine, and he recommended that men should not be admitted for the three-year course unless they had mastered the elements of Latin and Greek. To this raising of entrance standards the Council agreed, while approving that the Principal should be finally responsible for the selection of students. In February, 1901, the Rev. W. H. Barlow, D.D., was elected President of the Council in place of Dr. Peache, while the Rev. G. F. Whidborne and Mr. T. Cheney Garfit were elected Council members. It was proposed that a memorial fund should be opened for the College founder, to take the form of endowments for scholarships and exhibitions, and in after years men were proud to wear the distinctive red "button and cord" on the back of their college gowns, the mark of a Peache Scholar. As he was leaving London in the course of the year to become Dean of Peterborough, Dr. Barlow asked to be relieved of the office of Secretary to the Council which he had held for some fourteen years, and Prebendary J. F. Kitto was elected Secretary in his place.

The introductory period of Dr. Greenup's principalship (he had been made an honorary D.D. of the Western University of Canada in 1902) may be said to have ended in 1903, which also marked the fortieth anniversary of the College's foundation. By then further staff changes had taken place; in 1902, the Rev. E. H. Cox left to become Vice-Principal of St. Aidan's, Birkenhead, and the Rev. T. Allison to be domestic chaplain to the Bishop of Liverpool. On the Principal's recommendation, the Rev. C. S. Wallis, former student of the College, and the Rev. W. H. Brotherton were appointed tutors. In July, 1903, for the first time, the College was reported full with fifty-four resident students and six non-resident, and a reduction in the length of terms was agreed to, the Lent term to be eleven weeks, the Easter, ten weeks, and the Michaelmas, eleven—thirty-two weeks in all. Also in 1903 the Rev. J. B. M. Grimes was appointed tutor. He had been Gatford and Kaye Scholar of Jesus College, Cambridge, taking a second class in the Classical Tripos and a second class in the Theological Tripos, and was formerly curate of Northam, Devon. On the Council, the death of Prebendary Kitto brought the Rev. G. F. Whidborne to fill his place as Secretary, and the Rev. H. E. Fox, of C.M.S., Salisbury Square, to fill the vacancy. This year was also notable for the appointment of Bishop Taylor Smith as Chaplain-General to the Forces.

The Principal reported at the annual summer gathering that the Peache Memorial Fund had reached £7,000. He stated that he had instituted a regular Thursday evening chapel service, with visiting preachers, which has remained a feature of College life and worship ever since. Lectures in psychology and ethics had been added to the course. He stressed the main distinctive features of the College as being devotion to the study of Scripture, instruction in practical work, and loyal adherence to the Book of Common Prayer, making men Catholic, Protestant and Evangelical in outlook. He also referred with pleasure to the appointment of Dr. Wace as Dean of Canterbury.

But the following year Greenup underwent a long and serious illness, while at the same time he suffered a sad bereavement in the loss of his son, Cyril. His absence may well have had some effect upon College conduct and discipline, both among tutors and students, for the next three years were clouded by dissension between the Principal and his staff. Various charges were preferred against Greenup, and were heard by the Council. One tutor was dismissed, and others were asked to withdraw their accusation, the Council considering that they were either groundless or founded on misunderstandings. At this point the Bishop of London (Winnington Ingram) who had accepted the post of Visitor to the College, intervened, and the matter was laid before him. Meanwhile, the Principal and one tutor were carrying on the whole work, alone, except for the assistance of the external lecturers. On examining the correspondence, the Bishop reported that nothing in the case justified his interference on behalf of the tutors, but he expressed the hope that relationships between Principal and staff would quickly improve, as the matter must be well known to the students, and could not but have deleterious effects on the spiritual life of the college.

There is no doubt that Greenup was extremely unpopular with some of the students, though the Council steadily gave him their support in the whole unpleasant affair. To add to his difficulties at this time, the bad condition of the drains caused the complete closure of the College in the autumn of 1906. It was not surprising that in that year the numbers of students had dropped, with a falling off in income of £700. Only forty were resident in 1907, while, in order to balance receipts and expenditure, the average number of resident students had to be forty-five. On the brighter side, we find that in 1906 A. R. Whately, the former Vice-Principal, and now lecturer at the College, had obtained the first London University Doctor of Divinity degree for his thesis on *The Inner Light*, which was published in 1908.

Also in 1906, a familiar and well-loved name first appears, for the Rev. Harold Smith was then appointed Lecturer in Philosophy, thus beginning an association with the College lasting for exactly thirty years. He had been Naden Divinity Student of St. John's College, Cambridge, taking first classes in the Classical and Theological Triposes, gaining the Jeremie Septuagint Prize and the Crosse Scholarship. He had been Chaplain and Censor of King's College, London, and curate of Grimley, Worcestershire, before coming to Highbury. It seems difficult to believe that at first he was a suspect figure, and he was obliged to agree not to lecture in Old Testament "as his views were inclined towards those of the Higher Critics." But the Council left the nature of his employment to the Principal's discretion, and many generations of Johnians will rejoice that his views were considered sufficiently "safe" to secure his services for a long period. The whole question of sound doctrine was much in the minds of the Council and staff, even extending to the sports field, for a special resolution laid down that football should not be played with students of Kelham College! A most generous gift of £1,200 was accepted by the Council at this time from the executors of Alfred Roberts to found the exhibitions named after him, preference being given to men of limited means and to sons of clergy. The exhibition amounted to £21 a year for three years.

In 1907 Greenup was appointed Chairman of the Board of Examiners for the divinity degrees at London University for the ensuing year—a tribute to his widely recognised erudition as an Oriental language scholar. In the same year, the Rev. C. H. Gill was appointed tutor; late Exhibitioner of Jesus College, Oxford, he took a second class in Mathematical Moderations, and was Chaplain of Jesus College, and curate of St. Ebbe's, Oxford, from 1905 to 1907. Visiting lecturers included the Revs. H. F. Gaster and H. G. Harding.

A change of President of the Council occurred in 1908 with the death of the Dean of Peterborough, who, as it was recorded, "for twenty-seven years gave invaluable help as examiner of candidates." As a member, then Secretary, and finally President of the Council, Dr. Barlow had for a long time served the interests of the College and the Church as a whole in many fields. Prebendary Grose Hodge wrote in the course of an appreciation: "He had the greatest influence in Church patronage of any man in England—far greater than any bishop. . . . I have known him travel 300 miles and 300 miles back again to hear a man preach who had been recommended for a certain parish. He was a man who lived consciously in the presence of God." Dean Wace was appointed President of the Council in his place.

For some years a feeling had been growing among former students that the status of the Hall should be raised. It was expressed in a memorandum submitted to the Council by the Rev. S. A. Johnston, then Vicar of St. Mary's, Peckham. He pointed out that for forty-five years men had entered the ministry from Highbury without any degree, or even a diploma, unlike those ordained from King's College, London. He believed that the decline in College numbers was due to the fees being too high and the college status too low. The cost for the whole course was about £200, after passing the Central Examination. He pointed out that for the same cost men could obtain their L.Th. at Durham, with only one further examination to give them a B.A. He proposed making the normal standard for entry the matriculation examination of some approved university. The aim of teaching would be to obtain a degree in divinity for students leaving the College, which might mean a three or a four-year course. He proposed to effect financial economies in the course by obtaining additional funds through an appeal for subscriptions and donations to increase the endowment, especially from former College members. He felt that this would fulfil the aims of the founder and raise the educational standard of the College, and its theological status, as well as meeting the requirements of the Church of the day.

A committee to consider these proposals was therefore set up, consisting of Dean Wace, Lord Kinnaird, Canons Bernard, Girdlestone and Stuart, the Revs. J. E.Watts-Ditchfield and G. F.Whidborne, and Mr.W. G. Bradshaw, the Principal also attending. It met on July 27th, 1908. Dr. Greenup submitted a most important memorandum, in which he pointed out that the connection with London University was not very helpful, owing to the high standard required for degrees and the stringent conditions of residence and attendance at lectures. He also drew attention to the high overhead charges on the College: the rates, at £700 per annum, repairs averaging £300 to £400 per annum, and Dr. Waller's pension almost swallowed up the whole endowment. The building was ill-adapted for its purpose, long passages, large lecture-rooms, complicated heating apparatus and large grounds, all entailed enormous expense, including the employment of a gardener and carpenter at £160 per year. It was clear that some way must be found of lowering fees, and he suggested, as a temporary measure, the selling or letting of the playing field. But on the long-term view, it might be well to consider selling the present building, and building a Hall which could be run on more economical lines. He therefore made three propositions:

1. To move to one of the provincial universities, which he felt would be impractical, owing to the high fees required at Birmingham, Sheffield, or Leeds.
2. To move to Oxford or Cambridge, which would have many advantages, though he doubted whether they would be welcomed by the Cambridge authorities, who had a prejudice against new hostels.
3. To remain in London, in which case he urged the disposal of the present College buildings, and the acquiring of something smaller, envisaging residence for some thirty men.

The proposals both of Johnston and the Principal are significant—in the one case as foreshadowing the growing pressure which eventually led to the granting of the A.L.C.D.; and in the other case as being the first occasion among many when the Principal would advocate a move from Highbury. The Committee dismissed his first two suggestions, but on the third a number of ideas were put forward to attract men to the College; these included the selling of the College or the spare land; to amalgamate with the C.M. College at Islington; to sever connection with London University; and to require suitable students to take a two-or three-year course at Highbury, and then conclude with a year at Durham for the B.A. A subsequent Committee meeting in December,

1908, decided, by the Chairman's casting vote, to recommend to the Council the selling of the whole estate with a view to rebuilding elsewhere in the dioceses of London, Southwark or St. Albans. The Council, however, decided to take no action in the matter, even though Dr. Greenup's arguments were reinforced by the collapse of the wall on the west side of the chapel, which had to be rebuilt from the foundations. In addition, the long wall down Avenall Road "was afflicted by its annual sickness and needed a good deal of attention"!

Within two months, the President reported that he had seen the Bishop of London, who intimated that he was prepared to consider a three-year scheme of training with the Bishops of Southwark (E. S. Talbot) and St. Albans (Jacob). He much wished that Highbury men would take the London degree, but Dean Wace pointed out that this was impossible, owing to the high standard of that degree. Events behind the scenes took a dramatic turn in 1909. In March Mr. Bradshaw reported that he had received from the London County Council an offer of £40,000 for the College and grounds. The Council authorised the sale, and recommended rebuilding in the London Diocese, "the men to remain in residence for two years, and pass for the third year to a hostel at Durham" for the B.A. degree, where they would benefit from the influence of Bishop Moule and Dr. Gee. The sale of the college was confirmed by the Council in March. Two months later, the Rev. J. E. Watts-Ditchfield, Vicar of St. James the Less, Bethnal Green, an Old Johnian, who had been elected to the Council in June, 1908, and became its secretary in 1909, reported on a conversation he had had with Bishop Chavasse of Liverpool. The Bishop was not in favour of amalgamation with Wycliffe Hall, nor with erecting a new college at Oxford or Cambridge, but thought it best to find a site in the London area, and to secure a hostel at Durham, where a house was available. In June Mr. Bradshaw reported that plans had been sent in for a college to house seventy-two men, costing £29,000, leaving £10,000 for the surrounding land; enquiries were made as to Lord Grimthorpe's estate, "Batchwood," near St. Albans. Meanwhile, Mr. Watts-Ditchfield, with the Bishop's approval, had secured a good house for a hostel at Durham.

Then quite suddenly the picture changed. In July, Watts-Ditchfield, whose word carried great weight, said that, for old associations' sake, it would be better to see whether the present buildings could be adapted to a more economical working and the fees reduced. The architect also believed that it would be more economical to remain at

Highbury, and that alterations could be carried out whereby accommodation could be increased to eighty resident students at a cost of £7,000. The L.C.C. offer was therefore declined, and a reduction of fees agreed upon from £65 to £60 for sons of clergy and from £75 to £70 for others. One can only speculate as to the course of the college's history had its location been changed in 1909; in the light of future events, it would seem to have been a wise and economic move, but one is dealing with facts, not possibilities, and for another thirty years the familiar Highbury premises were retained.

References have been made to the securing of a house at Durham for use as a hostel for Highbury students. The Lambeth Conference of 1908 and Canterbury Convocation of 1909, both passed resolutions urging that the training of clergy should, whenever possible, include a degree in Arts. It was both for this and other reasons that the St. John's Hall Council decided to open a hostel to enable their men to take advantage of the Durham course. A house in the South Bailey (formerly known as Hatfield Lodge) was taken, and the foundation owed much to the generosity of Mr. W. G. Cruddas. St. John's Hall, Durham, as it was called, was formally opened and dedicated on October 12th, 1909, by the Bishop of Jarrow. The Bishop of Durham, the Dean of Canterbury, and the Dean of Durham were also present. It began with only five men, and the first Principal was the Rev. Sidney Nowell Rostron, of St. John's College, Cambridge, who took a first class in the Theological Tripos, with Hulsean, Naden Divinity, and Greek Testament prizes. In its second year numbers had increased to sixteen. He was succeeded in 1912 by Dr. Dawson Walker, who later became Canon of Durham and Professor of Divinity. The Church of St. Mary the Less was set aside for use as a college chapel. The fees were to be £59 per year. The Council of St. John's Hall, Highbury, was its governing body, with a small local council consisting of the Bishop of Jarrow, Dr. Dawson Walker, the Rev. J. How, and Mr. Heawood. On the relation between the two colleges, it was officially resolved (November 24th, 1909) that "St. John's Hall, Highbury, has a branch at Durham, called St. John's Hall, Durham, which is affiliated to the University, and students who have spent two years at Highbury after passing the Central Examination have the privilege of admission to the Hall at Durham in preference to other students." In 1910, another house was taken, and the work rapidly expanded. The trust deed provided for a council of twenty members, four representatives each from St. John's, Highbury, St. Aidan's, Birkenhead, and Durham University; two from the Church Missionary Society, and six co-opted members. The deed was drafted by Mr. W. Joynson Hicks (later Lord Brentford), who was now elected a member of the Highbury Council. In 1919, by authority of the Council of the Durham Colleges, the Hall assumed the title of College, and by 1923 it had become like St. Chad's, a constituent college of the university. The Council was reconstituted in 1922, the special representation being abolished, and a separate governing body being set up, so that the college became fully independent. For a long time, some men from St. John's used to take their degrees at Durham; or else the Durham L.Th. while at Highbury. In fact, the L.Th., and the rule whereby licentiates in theology were allowed to take the Durham B.A. degree after one year's residence, were only withdrawn in 1949.[1]

In view of the forthcoming jubilee of the College, Mr. Watts-Ditchfield suggested in 1910 that a public appeal should be made for funds to assist ordination candidates, and proposed a Million Shilling Fund to be raised in two years. This was duly launched, and by November, 1913, had raised £8,000. It was agreed that this should be divided between St. John's Highbury, St. John's, Durham, and St. Aidan's, Birkenhead, each receiving £2,500 apiece, the Highbury share to be expended on bursaries.

In July, 1911, the Rev. C. H. Gill resigned as tutor to become assistant missioner for the London Jews Society, and the Rev. S. H. Martin, formerly Scholar of Trinity College, Oxford, with a second class in Classics, and a second class in Lit. Hum., became tutor in his place. The Rev. J. N. Carpenter, formerly Principal of the theological college at Allahabad, was temporarily engaged as lecturer.

A further change occurred early in 1912 with the resignation of the Rev. C. S. Wallis on his appointment as Vice-Principal of St. John's Hall, Durham. The Council recorded their "high appreciation of his work and character, and also their warm thanks for the admirable services which he had rendered to the college." He was succeeded by the Rev. W. Dodgson Sykes, a Foundation Scholar of St. John's College, Cambridge, with a first class in the Theological Tripos, Part I, Hughes Prizeman, Naden Divinity Student, and Crosse Scholar—an outstanding academic record. For twenty years he was a well-loved figure at Highbury. Over £600 had been received from the Dean Barlow Memorial Fund; it was decided that this should be invested to bring in a sum of about £20 a year for an exhibition to be held for one year at Durham. A further difficulty loomed ahead. In November, 1912,

[1] See C. E. Whiting, *The University of Durham*, pp. 173f.

Dr. Wace reported to the Council an interview which he had had with the Archbishop of Canterbury on the question of degrees for ordination candidates. The Archbishop pointed out that as from 1917, the bishops would insist on all ordinands being graduates. Though this matter caused considerable alarm in all non-graduate colleges, the First World War prevented its being put into operation.

The Jubilee of the college was celebrated at a special reunion gathering at Highbury on May 7th, 1913; the address in chapel was given by Prebendary W. E. Burroughs, Rector of St. Peter's, Tiverton (father of the future Bishop of Ripon) on the theme "Stewards of God's grace" from I Pet. iv. 10 and 11. The retiring President of the union, the Rev. W. J. Watkins, took the chair at the business meeting, during the course of which he handed over his office to Prebendary Grose Hodge, and a high tribute was paid to the Secretary, F. Pring Rowe. At the dinner in the evening, speeches were made by the Principal, the President (Dean Wace), the Treasurer (Lord Kinnaird), and the Chaplain-General, Bishop Taylor Smith. The main address was given by Prebendary Grose Hodge on "Has the Evangelical School a future?" This he answered in the affirmative because of the acceptance it gave to the authority of Scripture; because it faced the fact of sin; it preached a full gospel, and had great missionary zeal. Papers were also read by the Revs. G. E. Ford and H. Montague Dale.

The main jubilee meeting was held on June 6th at Church House, Westminster, with the Archbishop of Canterbury in the chair. After the Rev. J. E. Watts-Ditchfield had read a statement dealing with the history of the College, the Archbishop, in the course of his speech, paid tribute to the college staff, who had worked "to raise the common standard, and make the average parish clergyman a fitter instrument for the work with which God entrusts him." He concluded: "I myself bless God for the good service which you in St. John's Hall have rendered for these fifty years." Other speakers included the Bishop of Norwich (Pollock), who had asked to be present because he was a godson of Miss Peache, and was born within a few months of the College's foundation; the Bishop of Kensington (J. P. Maud), the Dean of Canterbury, and Mr. W. Joynson Hicks, M.P. At the evening dinner at the Holborn Restaurant at which over ninety were present, speeches were made by Mr. T. W. H. Inskip, Bishop Taylor Smith, and the Rev. S. A. Johnston; Dr. Eugene Stock proposed the toast of "the College and Staff," to which the Principal responded, while in response to the toast of "Our Guests," Dr. Guy Warman, Principal of St. Aidan's, Birkenhead, remarked on the decision of the Bishops to postpone for three years their requirement of a degree for all ordinands; he prophesied (correctly) that postponement would in fact mean cancellation of this decision. The jubilee celebrations concluded with a garden party in the college grounds on June 26th.

By 1913, over a thousand men had passed through St. John's Hall, while the Clerical Union had given splendid support to their old college, having raised more than £10,000, including £2,000 to the college completion fund, and £7,500 towards a memorial to Dr. Peache. They also marked the occasion of the jubilee by presenting a new lectern to the College chapel.

A few months before the jubilee, the Council had sanctioned the appointment of Vice-Presidents, and those first invited to fill this office were the Bishops of Durham, Liverpool and Ripon, and Sir John Kennaway, who had just resigned from the Council.

It was at the end of 1912 that Mr. (later, Sir) Henry Norris, Director of the Woolwich Arsenal Football Club, a builder, and Mayor of Fulham, looked around for fresh premises. The club was at a low ebb and a move to a fresh locality was felt essential to revive its fortunes. He therefore approached Mr. Bradshaw of the College Council with an offer to purchase the six and a half acres of the college grounds to be used for professional football matches at a cost of £10,000. The Council offered a lease of this land for twenty-one years at a rent of £700 a year, rising by £100 a year to £1,000 for the remainder of the term, and the club agreed to admit staff and students free to their league matches. It also proposed to build a grandstand and dressing-room on the east side.

When this proposal became known, early in 1913, there was a violent reaction by Highbury residents, who feared that the peace of the neighbourhood would be destroyed, and from the congregation of St. John's Church. The evils of professional football were stressed as having a bad effect on the young people of the district. Many letters of protest were sent by local residents to the Council Secretary, and it was reported that the Borough Council were preparing to apply for a court injunction to restrain such development. The Vicar of Islington had also joined in the protest. The Council thereupon unanimously requested Mr. Bradshaw to withdraw from the whole proposal if possible. He pointed out, however, that the matter had now gone too far to withdraw, and on a vote it was decided by four votes to three that the lease agreement should be signed, but a clause was inserted stipulating that no football should be played on Sundays, Good Friday or Easter Day. In June, 1914, a cricket pitch was secured free of charge in Finsbury Park two days a week.

Just nine years later, in 1923, Sir Henry Norris offered £25,000 for the purchase of the football field, and certain other ground for a further £1,868. To this the Council agreed, together with a lease of the tennis courts (known in the College as "the cabbage patch") for a practice ground at an annual rental of £100 a year for twenty-one years, subject to the students being allowed access to it when not otherwise in use. From September 29th, 1924, when the agreement became operative, the college became a "tenant" of the Arsenal Football Club on an eighty-year lease, until the lease was surrendered by the College, with suitable compensation, as from December 25th, 1945. In 1925 the club issued 100 tickets for staff and students to attend club matches, which were reduced to fifty five years later. In the "mighty Arsenal" period of the '30s, many will remember watching such stars as Hume, Bastin, Drake, and Alex James, Male and Hapgood, Crayston and Copping (all internationals), and the notorious match against Italy in October, 1934 (which some watched from the college roof!), when the club created a record by supplying seven members of the England side, and, despite several unfortunate incidents, England won 3-2. Many whose interest had been aroused in the club's fortunes during their time at College remained "Arsenal fans" for years afterwards.

But to return to the jubilee year. In June the Rev. Harold Smith, who had been a lecturer since 1906, was appointed full-time tutor, while Mr. T. W. H. Inskip (later Lord Caldecote) became a member of the Council in place of the Rt. Hon. James Round. In February, 1914, the Rev. J. M. Harden, B.D., LL.D., Headmaster of Kilkenny College, "a man of learning, ability, and spiritual power" in the Principal's words, was appointed Vice-Principal. A matter of great satisfaction to the College at this time was the appointment of the first Old Johnian to an English diocesan bishopric, the Clerical Secretary, the Rev. J. E. Watts-Ditchfield, becoming the first Bishop of Chelmsford. The Council recorded "their grateful sense of the admirable services rendered by him to St. John's Hall, not only as Secretary but previously. His advice has always been of great value to them, and they appreciate deeply the spiritual energy and devoted labour with which he has constantly promoted the interests of the College." They were glad to appoint him a Vice-President. At the same time the Rev. T. J.

Pulvertaft and Mr. A. R. Buxton were elected Council members, the former succeeding Watts-Ditchfield as Secretary. In November, 1914, Mr. Joynson Hicks resigned and was made Vice-President; the Rev. Harrington Lees and Mr. W. H. Patchell became members.

On the question of relationships with London University, the Principal reported in June that he with others had had an interview with the University authorities, pleading that the University examinations might be adjusted to allow men attending theological colleges like St. John's to take the London B.A. degree, but no satisfaction was gained. Once more the question came up as to whether it would be advisable to move the college to Oxford or Cambridge, but it was decided to take no action for the present.

Seventy-one men were in residence in the autumn of 1914, but with the outbreak of war numbers naturally declined. Indeed, the Council recommended the Principal to use his discretion about accepting men of military age, and he reported that a number had deferred their training until after the war in order to undertake military service.

An inspection of the College on behalf of the Advisory Council of Training for the Ministry took place in November, 1914, and the report of the inspectors is important as indicating the opinions of impartial observers as to the position of the College at the outbreak of the war. Drs. Rendall (lately Headmaster of Charterhouse) and Joyce (Warden of St. Deiniol's Library, Hawarden) regarded the staff as adequate and the devotional training admirable, while the training in pastoralia covered a wide field and gave a valuable insight into parochial work. But they severely criticised the time wasted in consequence of the character of the examinations that must be passed, and proceeded:

> "Recent University reform has steadily aimed at associating examination tests with the lines of actual teaching. In theological colleges where it would have special advantages, no such relation is as yet admitted. . . . The regimen of St. John's Hall is in all respects comparable with that which leads up to the A.K.C., and the net results furnish a much more complete index of fitness and capacity than the bare class lists of the University Preliminary Examination. Authoritively issued and tabulated, and correlated with those of cognate colleges, they would be entitled to something of the same recognition as is in practice accorded to the King's College Associateship."

In discussing the relationship with London University, attention was called to the absence of any B.A. course suitable to theological students, whereas with an appropriate degree course the difficulty, mainly financial, should not be beyond the power of the Church to meet.

St. John's Hall, London College of Divinity.

The Hostel and
Gateway,
St. John's Hall.

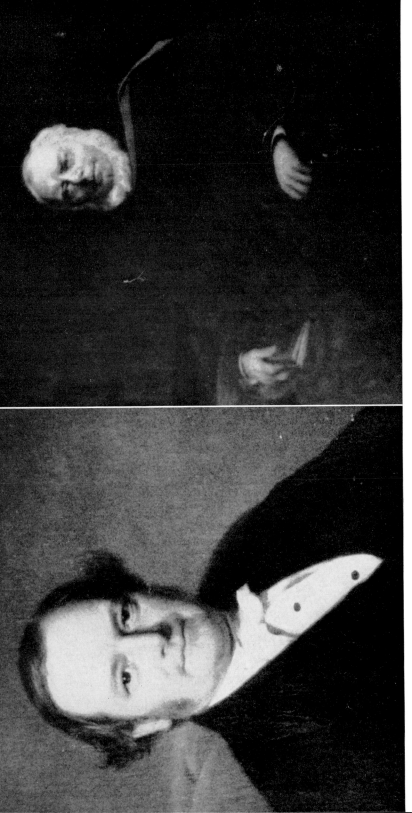

The First Principal,
the Rev. Thomas Parnall Boultbee, LL.D.

The Founder, Alfred Peache.

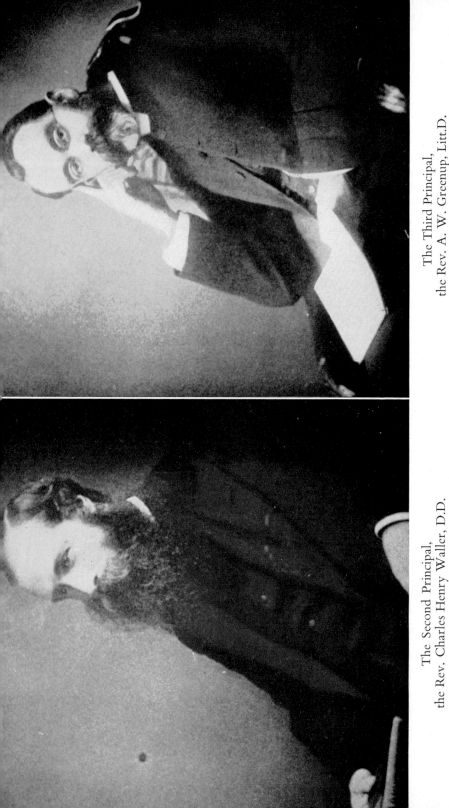

The Second Principal,
the Rev. Charles Henry Waller, D.D.

The Third Principal,
the Rev. A. W. Greenup, Litt.D.

The addition of a fourth year to the course would put it on financial grounds beyond the reach of a large number of men. The College and grounds commanded praise, and it was felt that gain rather than loss had resulted from the lease of part of the grounds to the Woolwich Arsenal Football Club. They paid a high compliment to the devotion and administrative gifts of the Principal, but suggested that in general, secretarial assistance and postal and travelling expenses should be provided for college principals. As a result of this report, the central advisory committee recommended St. John's Hall for recognition by the bishops.

An addition to the staff at this time was the arrival of the Rev. J. N. Carpenter (who had obtained a London D.D. in November, 1914) as temporary tutor. Numbers dropped to forty-nine at the end of 1915, when eighteen students were serving with the Forces. As a consequence of the Zeppelin airship raid in September, 1915, the College was insured against aircraft damage. As far as the men were concerned, the Council felt that the matter of military service must be left to their own decision, in consultation with the Principal. Mr. Sykes was asked to remain as tutor, because, when conscription came into force, an order was issued early in 1916 by the War Office that theological students were to be exempted from military service if they desired, and work was still carried on, though with much reduced numbers.

The much-publicised National Mission of Repentance and Hope held in 1916 brought a widely welcomed opportunity of practical work, and the students gave enthusiastic assistance to the special gatherings arranged in the neighbouring parishes. By the spring of 1917, conditions were becoming extremely difficult, and the Principal reported that fuel supplies were inadequate. Only thirteen students were in residence at the end of that year, dropping to eight in 1918. Owing to the small numbers, the chapel and dining-hall had been closed, one of the lecture-rooms being used for the dining-hall, and services held in the reading-room. A Council member, Mr. A. R. Buxton, was killed in France, but three former students were decorated for gallantry, the Revs. A. T. Morgan and H. Richards gaining the M.C., and S. J. Delight the D.C.M., having been recommended for the V.C.

With the war ended, the College was faced with a programme of urgent repairs. The roof was in very bad condition, and the heating apparatus needed thorough overhaul. The hostel walls needed underpinning, and a number of bedrooms were spoilt through rain coming in. Accordingly repairs were put in hand, at a cost of £900. Numbers rose sharply in 1919, fifty-one students being in residence for the Summer Term. The Principal, however, was not hopeful of a large increase in numbers, owing to the strong competition offered by the newly-formed Test School at Knutsford. He suggested that an associateship in theology should be conferred on successful students of the Hall, similar to the A.K.C. The Rev. Harold Smith had obtained his London D.D. for his thesis on the "Ante-Nicene Exegesis of the Gospels," and the title of Professor of Philosophy was conferred on him, and that of Professor of Systematic Theology on Dr. Harden.

Staff changes in 1919 and 1920 included the resignation of Prebendary Grose Hodge from the Whitehead Professorship after twenty-one years on his becoming Rector of Birmingham, and his succession by Prebendary W. H. Stone, Rector of Chipstead, Surrey. Barely a year later, however, Prebendary Stone died, and the Rev. the Hon. W. Talbot Rice, Vicar of St. Paul's, Onslow Square, was elected in his place, while the Rev. B. W. Horan, B.D., from Trinity College, Dublin, was appointed tutor. The Bishop of Barking (J. T. Inskip) and Mr. S. H. Gladstone were elected to the College Council.

On October 12th, 1920, the Dean of Canterbury unveiled in the college chapel a bronze memorial tablet to those students of St. John's Hall who fell in the war, in which sixty-one students had served. Its inscription read as follows:

"To the glory of Christ crucified; In honour of the men of this Hall who died in the Great War, 1914-1919.

F. W. Ainley	R. F. Johnson
W. Brown.	E. H. H. Lough
C. P. Burdett	P. A. Newell
J. C. Cross	R. W. Park
L. Hartley	S. D. Sumner

The address was given by the Bishop of Chelmsford.

Meanwhile, it was clear that certain changes would be needed to bring the College curriculum into line with developments in other theological colleges. A proposal was therefore adopted that the staffs of St. John's and King's College should meet to discuss the possibility of outlining a course for a common final examination. The meeting took place in June, 1921, the King's representatives being led by the Rev. (later Dean) W. R. Matthews, and the principle of joint examinations was accepted. Consultations continued in the autumn of 1921, when certain resolutions were passed. These included an agreement by King's to conduct jointly an internal final examination for the students of both colleges at the end of their third year. It should consist of papers on Christian theology, Old and New Testament, Greek Testament, Prayer Book, and Ecclesiastical History, together with voluntary papers in Hebrew or Philosophy. The syllabus was to be arranged by the teaching staffs of the two colleges, with the approval of their governing bodies, the examiners to be members of each teaching staff together with an external examiner. Set books were to be the same for both colleges, and should be related to those required for the London B.D. So far as King's was concerned, the proposed examination would be accepted as equivalent to the third-year examination for the A.K.C., provided a student's previous examinations had been satisfactory.

In June, 1922, the President stated that a Committee set up to deal with College reorganisation had reported that it was not necessary or desirable for St. John's to prepare internal students for the London B.D., but that it was essential that external students should be received for that examination. The Committee rightly felt that it was most important that the College should be on the same academic level as other London theological colleges, especially King's. Early in 1923 the Examination Committee approved the scheme for the joint final examination as to syllabus, stipulating that an examiner appointed by the newly-termed Central Advisory Council for Training for the Ministry should take part in the College examinations at the end of the first and second years. By June it was reported that C.A.C.T.M. had passed the proposals for the joint final examination for the two colleges, while Durham University agreed to accept this examination in lieu of the final L.Th. These important steps, the result of protracted discussions, removed any danger of St. John's being isolated from current development in clergy training. In particular, the close association with King's reinforced the arguments for the eventual granting of some tangible recognition for St. John's men who had successfully completed their course, so strengthening the claim for an associateship on a par with the A.K.C.

Meanwhile, the College was experiencing a most difficult financial period, and for this and other reasons the Principal once again set before the Council in July, 1921, a memorandum on the desirability of moving to a provincial university centre. He felt once again the necessity of this, partly because of the increase of rates (£745 per annum in 1910; £1,476 in 1920) and the difficulties in the way of students obtaining arts degrees. He also mentioned the growing desire among laymen that candidates for the Ministry should be educated alongside students entering other professions. At a provincial university, theological and other students would sit beside each other in the same classroom. The unsuitability of the college premises was another factor. Sentiment, the opposition of some old students, and the loss of a grant from the Parochial Charities were the only reasons in favour of remaining in London. He suggested a move to Bristol or Reading, at either of which he believed theological students would be welcomed. This, however, the Council rejected, and instead proposed a reduction in professional staff, despite the Principal's strong disagreement. On the departure of the Rev. B. W. Horan to take up a post at Wycliffe College, Toronto, it was decided that his place should not be filled.

Changes on the Council in 1922 brought the elections of the Rev. H. W. Hinde, Vicar of Islington, and of Prebendary Grose Hodge. Lord Kinnaird also resigned from the Council and from the post of treasurer, being succeeded by Mr. W. G. Bradshaw. On the staff, the Vice-Principal, Dr. Harden resigned after eight years to become Head-master of King's Hospital School, Dublin, and was succeeded by Mr. Dodgson Sykes; in February, 1923, the appointment was confirmed as Junior Tutor of the Rev. O. A. C. Irwin, B.D., of Trinity College, Dublin, formerly curate of St. Cuthbert's, West Hampstead.

His impressions of the College at this time make interesting reading. Of the fifty or so men, several had been in the Services, including a former major and lieutenant-commander. The spirit of devotion throughout the College was deep and sincere. In addition to the regular morning and evening prayer in chapel, some students met for prayer meetings before breakfast and rather more for prayer after dinner in hall. There was also a "wing" prayer meeting in each of the College wings, held in each student's study in turn, and a general College prayer meeting on Saturday evenings. The students in general were strongly Protestant in character, though a few tended towards Anglo-Catholicism. Some men still believed in the ultra-literal interpretation of the Bible, including the acceptance of Creation in six twenty-four hour days. The College had a branch of the Student Christian Movement but the newly-founded London Inter-Faculty Christian Union was making headway, especially through the influence of men who had come from B.C.M.S. parishes. Attendance at morning and evening prayer was, of course, compulsory; men arriving late came in by the side door and sat in some pews known locally as "the cab rank." On the whole, the College may be said to have presented a fairly harmonious appearance, though there were certain underlying tensions of which insufficient notice was taken.

The deaths within five months (August, 1923, and January, 1924) of Bishop Watts-Ditchfield and Dean Wace brought great sorrow to the Council, who passed special resolutions expressing their debt to those who had done so much for the welfare of the College. Bishop Watts-Ditchfield "wholeheartedly devoted himself to the interests of the College, and never spared himself in working for its welfare." He was "a beloved colleague" and "a true and constant friend." Dean Wace had been a Council member for twenty-five years, and its President for fifteen, and his colleagues expressed their gratitude to God for what He had accomplished through his servant.

The silver jubilee of Dr. Greenup's appointment as Principal was reached in March, 1924, and the Bishop of London preached in the College chapel to mark the occasion. Financial difficulties were continuing, and within the Council there was some support for the Principal's proposal that the College should be moved to Reading. Mrs. Greenup was also calling attention to the difficulty of obtaining domestic staff, and to the absence of labour-saving devices. As a result, wages were increased, the hot-water supply improved, and some showers were installed for students.

A visit by C.A.C.T.M. inspectors (Bishop Linton Smith of Hereford and Canon G. W. Evans) in December, 1923, however, brought a report which called for serious consideration. They had stayed in the College for two days, attending some lectures, and making a thorough investigation of its administration and academic work, on which they made a number of adverse criticisms. They recommended closer ties with London University, which it was hoped would emphasise the need to secure for the abler men the prospect of obtaining degrees in divinity. The University authorities replied to the report by expressing the hope that their new Diploma in Theology would help to this end. But no proposals were put forward on the question of making it easier for Highbury men, however able, to satisfy the requirements for a London degree.

In order to convey the College property to the Arsenal Football Club, in May, 1924, the Council were obliged, under an Act of 1872, to register as a charity. From this time, its official title was "The Governors of St. John's College of Divinity registered." The Bishop of Barking (J. T. Inskip) was now elected President, and vacancies on the

Council were filled by the Rev. T. W. Gilbert, D.D., Rector of Bradfield, Berkshire, the Rev. H. F. S. Adams, Vicar of Holy Trinity, Redhill, Surrey, and Mr. Albert Mitchell.

The situation in the college deteriorated in many respects during the academic year 1924-5. No student was reading for the B.D. Only forty men were in residence; there was much illness, and the domestic staff was inadequate. There had been several robberies, the housekeeper having had a bag snatched from her containing £3 of College money, while from the background came the threat that Bishop Burrows of Chichester and Dr. Hicks, President and Secretary respectively of C.A.C.T.M., were advocating the abolition of non-graduate colleges. In June, 1925, Dr. Greenup sent in another memorandum to the Council recommending the discontinuance of all connection with London University, because the London degrees were beyond the capacity of most of the men, and the strain on the staff in preparing only a few men was undesirable. In twenty-five years only seven men had taken the B.D. The connection with King's College for the final examination was a private agreement, and that examination was not recognised by the University; neither was the new Diploma in Theology examination of assistance, as it was not recognised by the bishops. He felt that it was of prime importance that the affiliation with Durham should be continued until the College should move to Cambridge or some place where men could get a degree on reasonable terms. He then reported that he had been offered the living of Great Oakley by his old College, St. John's, Cambridge, which he had accepted, and therefore tendered his resignation as Principal.

The Council, in accepting his resignation, expressed their appreciation of all that Dr. Greenup had done for the College as "a loyal teacher of the Evangelical faith"; they also paid tribute to the devoted services of Mrs. Greenup and "her ceaseless oversight of the students, who owe to her sympathetic care a debt of gratitude which they have frequently expressed."

Dr. Greenup retired from Great Oakley in 1931, and went to live near Basingstoke until his death in 1952 at the age of eight-five.

It should be recognised that Dr. Greenup's real life-work lay in the field of Rabbinics, for he was widely known as a Hebrew scholar. The list of his Hebrew studies, many of them translations, fills some twenty lines in *Crockford's Clerical Directory*. He was awarded the degree of Doctor of Letters by Trinity College, Dublin, in 1909. Before his appointment to St. John's, he had co-operated with Dr.

W. F. Moulton between 1895 and 1898 in bringing out a complete edition of the Revised Version, Greenup's part being concerned with the marginal references. Moulton recorded his "great satisfaction with the admirable way in which Mr. Greenup had done his work." As *The Times* obituary noted, "his career was closely bound up with the Theological Faculty of the University of London, of which he was Dean fron 1908 to 1912." He was an examiner in theology at Cambridge in 1898, in 1909-10, and in 1924, and at London in Hebrew and Greek Testament from 1903 to 1912 and from 1922 to 1924; also in ecclesiastical history in 1905-6, and in Hebrew and Syriac from 1924-46. He acted as examiner in these subjects at Liverpool and Durham. He resumed teaching in 1932 as Professor of Biblical Languages at the B.C.M.S. College, Bristol, a position he held until 1947. His great learning continued to be his abiding interest, and until a few months before his death, the Hebrew and Greek Scriptures were his constant companions. His first senior student, C. H. Winter, who remained his close friend, has paid the most affectionate tribute to his memory. He was "not only a diligent student and clever tutor, but above all else a man of faith and prayer. This spirit, gendered by the Principal, became the formative element in the lives of over 500 who were trained by him." He was a keen cricketer, and it was at his suggestion that the Hockey Club was formed. Neither was he above donning a top-hat before kicking off for a Shield final Soccer match. Modest and unassuming, he carried his learning lightly, so that he was frequently able to raise a laugh during his lectures. His sense of humour was also much in evidence outside the classroom. On one occasion, a small group of men decided to instal the college donkey in the bedroom of an unpopular student. This involved pushing and tugging the unfortunate animal up a stone staircase. During this process, the door of the Principal's study opened, and he passed the foot of the stairs. Glancing upwards, he paused and said: "Be kind to your poor brother, gentlemen!" The incident was abruptly closed. In his own field of study, he was a figure of international repute, contributing to many English and foreign journals, though his work could be fully appreciated only by a select band of scholars. Both Dr. and Mrs. Greenup opened their home unreservedly to students, many of whom still look back with pleasure to the "happy and devotional Sunday evenings" spent in their company.

As a Principal his achievement is more difficult to assess. He encountered considerable opposition at times from his staff, from disagreement over his policies, and he had to contend with the immense problems raised by the outbreak and course of the First World War, and those of reorganisation after it had ended. Moreover, it is clear that his personal wish, for many reasons and for many years, was to move the College from Highbury—a suggestion always rejected by the Council, whose members on a number of occasions do not appear to have taken much trouble to understand his point of view. There is no doubt that discipline in the College could have been improved, particularly in the post-war years. But the text of his first sermon in the College chapel best indicates the basic principle which he always endeavoured to set before his students: "Whatsoever thy hand findeth to do, do it with all thy might."

CHAPTER IV

Maturity and Achievement, 1926-42

THE year 1925-6 was one of suspense, which reacted unfavourably on the life of the College. The Council requested the Vice-Principal, Mr. Dodgson Sykes, to take charge until the arrival of a new Principal, and it was not anticipated that the new appointment would be long delayed. Indeed, urgency was increased by two reports received from the inspectors of London University and from C.A.C.T.M. Both bodies recommended considerable reforms and reorganisation in the work of the College, but felt it wiser that the changes necessary should be made by a new Principal. In October Mr. Sykes reported fifty-five men in residence; he had obtained temporary assistance on the teaching staff from the Revs. H. V. Edmunds and E. G. Bevan.

The long interregnum was entirely due to most serious disagreement among Council members as to the choice of a new Principal. Nine meetings were held to discuss the matter between October, 1925, and May, 1926. By February stalemate had been reached, no candidate obtaining the necessary two-thirds majority of votes. Five new Council members were elected in an effort to break the deadlock, and the original short list of three abandoned. Twenty-two names were now considered, after advertisements had been placed in the Church newspapers and in *The Times*. A short list of four was prepared, but on a vote the same division appeared, with equal numbers voting for the first two candidates. It was therefore decided that a simple majority vote must suffice, and on this being approved the Rev. T. W. Gilbert, D.D., Rector of Bradfield, Berkshire, was nominated Principal on May, 5th, 1926. Before his election was confirmed, however, the Council required him to send them a statement declaring his adherence to the Protestant and Evangelical principles of the Church of England, and his views on Old Testament criticism. With this before them, the Council confirmed the nomination, and Dr. Gilbert was formally elected Principal. He had had a distinguished career, gaining a first class in Modern History while at Balliol College, Oxford, taking his B.D. in 1912, and D.D. in 1923. Hitherto, he had exercised a pastoral ministry, with incumbencies at Colchester, St. Clement's, Oxford, and Bradfield, and he brought a wealth of parochial experience to his new and responsible post. It was not surprising that the differences on the Council had become known in the College, thus arousing certain tensions among the men. It was hard going for Sykes, who, in addition to the administrative burden, had the misfortune to damage his knee at football. He did his utmost in trying circumstances to keep things going, but the protracted delay in announcing the choice of a new Principal was undoubtedly a considerable strain upon him.

Changes on the Council at this period included the election of the Bishop of Chelmsford (Dr. H. A. Wilson), the Revs. G. T. Manley, and S. Nowell Rostron, and Messrs. A. G. Pite and M. Buxton. The resignation of the Rev. T. J. Pulvertaft from the Secretaryship was received with much regret, and appreciation expressed of his services during the previous twelve years, during which his "boundless energy, and unselfish devotion to the affairs of the College" were gratefully recorded. The Rev. H. W. Hinde was appointed in his place. On the recommendation of the new Principal, the Rev. E. G. Bevan was appointed resident tutor. A former student of the College and a London University B.D., he had previously been curate of St. Paul's Plumstead. The Rev. O. A. C. Irwin was appointed Bursar. Dr. Gilbert was installed as Principal on September 29th, 1926, and quickly set about tackling the many problems confronting him. He arrived to find a College much divided after the long interregnum, and he had to face the fact that many disapproved of his appointment. He never shirked these issues, but both he and Mrs. Gilbert, who supported him devotedly, had an uphill task at first to win the confidence and friendship of some of the College authorities, while among the students it was no secret that many would have preferred another Principal. With characteristic energy and resolution, Dr. Gilbert tightened up discipline, and with sanctified common sense turned a blind eye to minor incidents, so that before long he had won at least the respect of those who realised that here was a man of determination and ability, under whose guidance the College could look forward to new and higher attainments.

Practical matters were at once taken in hand; in 1927, electric light was installed throughout the whole College, and the financial position improved. The cost of maintenance per head for sixty-five students in 1926 was £68, but Dr. Gilbert reported that in 1927 for eighty-three students it was only £56 per head. A special sub-committee appointed to look into the relationship of the College with London University reported that so far as possible, all members of the tutorial staff should seek to become "recognised teachers" of the University. They approved Dr. Gilbert's policy of increasing the number of men who should enter for the London B.D. or some other degree, and the Principal was authorised to inform the Senate to this effect. At the same time the Secretary was requested to send in a memorandum on the advantages and disadvantages of moving the college from London, but it was decided that for the present at least no action should be taken. During his first two years the Prayer Book revision debates were a burning issue. Dr. Gilbert called the College together and carefully explained his own attitude to the new proposals. There were few students then who did not support him in general, so far as they understood the complicated issues involved.

Among other changes in the college, Dr. Gilbert arranged chapel services at 7.30 a.m. and 9.30 p.m., except on Thursdays, when, as previously, there was a visiting or staff preacher at evensong at 5.30 p.m. He took choir practices himself, and, though technically no musician, he raised the standard of singing, his "No *rallentando* in the last line" being a well-known directive, accompanied by decisive beats of his conductor's baton! An additional member of the staff, who joined at Michaelmas, 1927, was H. L. Ellison, who had been a student the previous term, and was ordained to this appointment.

In 1928 the College lost by the death of Prebendary Grose Hodge one who had been closely identified with Highbury for a longer period than anyone. A student in 1876, he was later President of the Cambridge Union. He was for twenty-two years Whitehead Professor, and had been a member of the Council for the six years before his death. He had also been President of the Old Johnians' Association. He was always proud of his connection with the College, and was a regular attendant at the reunion gatherings.

It was also in 1928 that the Council Secretary, the Rev. H. W. Hinde, Vicar of Islington, was appointed a Prebendary of St. Paul's. The Revs. A. E. Richardson, D.D., and T. G. Mohan were elected to the Council in 1929. During this year fairly extensive renovation was carried out on the chapel; the ceiling was cleaned and varnished, and the upper walls and pillars cleaned and painted. Financially, the college was now in a very sound position, and the number of students continued to rise, so that numbers touched 110 in the Michaelmas Term, 1929, several additional applicants being refused owing to inability to accommodate them in lodgings anywhere near the College. It is clear that within three years the new Principal had stamped the impression of his personality upon the life of the College. The main ingredients in tightening up discipline were a rigid enforcement of a few simple rules: in particular, compulsory chapel at 7.30 a.m.; keeping to one's rooms for prayer and Bible reading for half an hour after breakfast (it was most discomfiting to be found in Common Room during that period), and compulsory lectures.

Confidence in Dr. Gilbert both as teacher and administrator was high, as was shown by his appointment in 1930 as Chairman of the Faculty of Theology in London University. It was also learned with great satisfaction that Dr. Harold Smith had been appointed a Fellow of King's College, London. In the autumn, the Rev. A. R. Winnett, who had obtained a first class Honours London B.D. in the study of religion, became part-time lecturer, while the Rev. Martin Parsons, who obtained a second class in Part II of the History Tripos at Cambridge, joined the staff as resident tutor. The Rev. the Hon. W. Talbot Rice resigned as Whitehead Professor, a post he had held for ten years. He had great charm of manner, an alert and vigorous mind, and was a stimulating lecturer. He was succeeded by the Rev. S. Nowell Rostron, Vicar of St. James's, Paddington, after three years as Principal of St. John's College, Durham. He now resigned his seat on the Council. In March, 1931, the Rev. O. A. C. Irwin resigned to become Editorial Secretary of the C.M.S. after some eight years as tutor, combined for the last five with the office of Bursar. The same year saw the Rev. F. Bate, D.D., General Secretary of the Colonial and Continental Church Society, Mr. A. B. Keith and Commander R. G. Studd, D.S.O., elected to the Council, while Dr. Gilbert became a Proctor in Convocation; he was also appointed an examiner in higher degrees at London University. In the summer of 1932 the Vice-Principal, Dodgson Sykes, left to become Principal of the newly formed Bible Churchman's Missionary College at Bristol. He had been associated with Highbury for twenty years, broken by one year's service as an Army chaplain, and had endeared himself to a succession of students. At the annual reunion in September, Mr. Sykes was presented with an illuminated album containing a list of all subscribers, together with an accompanying cheque, and deep gratitude was expressed for all his past services to the College, not least on the sports field, together with good wishes for his new work at Bristol.

He was succeeded for a brief period by the Rev. B. W. Horan from Wycliffe College, Toronto, and in 1933 by the Rev. E. G. Bevan. The Rev. S. C. Steer was appointed tutor. He had obtained a first class in Greek and philosophy at Saskatoon University. The experiment was tried of appointing a student tutor, Mr. R. J. Cobb, who had obtained a second class in the Theological Tripos at Cambridge, being selected in 1933. An inspection of the College by Canon S. L. Brown, D.D., and the Ven. J. W. Hunkin, Archdeacon of Coventry (the first since the adverse report of 1924), was carried out in the Summer Term of 1932. In marked contrast to the criticisms of that report, the examiners were most favourably impressed with the work and academic standards of the college, noting particularly that matters which had received unfavourable comment had now been greatly improved. They concluded:

"We should like to congratulate the governing Body on the flourishing state of the College, and on the really splendid work which it is doing. This report may seem to be unduly complimentary, but our impressions are such that we feel we cannot help but say what we have said."

Such high commendation reflected the greatest credit on the Principal and on the whole teaching staff, and provided a striking tribute to the intellectual and devotional life of the College under the inspiring leadership of Dr. Gilbert.

The student body was a large and extremely varied one, drawn from many backgrounds. There were a number of men from public schools, often sons of clergymen, including a few graduates; others were from more humble social and educational origins. In addition, there were a few older men, who were taking shortened courses. Among these could be found at different periods a doctor, one or two schoolmasters, a miner, some who had served in the Forces, a planter from Ceylon, and Mr. Winston Churchill's former private detective. This diversity helped to correct the narrowness which is alleged to be a characteristic of some theological colleges. During this time the College was full to overflowing. Only graduates, who worked for the General Ordination Examination, and third-year men had studies to themselves, and a dozen or more had to be housed in lodgings (arranged by the Principal himself in a house-to-house canvass) in the neighbourhood. There were really too many students for a family feeling to develop. Indeed, the organisation of the College was geared to produce the opposite effect. It was a society in which there were layers, each annual intake of students being separate from the previous "year." Freshmen viewed the second-year men with respect, and both years dared not venture to occupy one of the eight armchairs in the Common Room if a third-year man came in sight. The Senior Student, nominated by the Principal, not elected by the men, was regarded with something approaching reverence, and no student ever left lecture-room, dining-hall or chapel before him. This regard for the office lay in the fact that its occupant acted as a liaison between the student body and the resident tutorial staff, including the Principal. The staff lived in their own world; apart from sharing students' tea and supper, they sat at a high table to which no student was ever invited. For conversation with the Principal, it was necessary for students to queue outside his study door at stated hours (the Senior Student could jump the queue), so, whether by accident or design, men discovered what a hierarchical society is like. On the whole, men had to make their way as best they could in this community. There was no chaplain to whom they could take spiritual or personal problems, and they had to learn to stand on their own feet. This produced breakdowns in some, and independence in most.

It was, of course, an evangelical College, but, apart from the aggressively "Protestant" appearance of the chapel, no attempt was made to mould students in an evangelical pattern. Provided a student conformed, nothing more would be asked of him. If this meant that the spiritual life of the College tended to be "flat," there was at least a sober, unemotional background, against which students could argue out their differences and develop their viewpoints. In general, the lecturers during the '30's accepted the "higher critical" attitude to the Scriptures without question. If the teaching given during those years is to be criticised, it would be for the method of imparting it (lectures were often dictation classes), and for its dry, academic nature. The content of the teaching was not old-fashioned; it was modern; indeed, it had to be, because the College course was stiffened by the B.D. course, which had to conform to the standards of scholarship required by the University of London. If Griffith Thomas on the Articles was the orthodox textbook, "Bicknell" was to be found on many men's shelves.

The atmosphere of the College was not strikingly pious, though there were groups within the College which adhered to definitely

78

B.C.M.S. or "liberal" views. A man might choose his own group, but was equally free to be independent. There was a good deal of ragging and practical joking, and to be called upon suddenly to make a speech in hall at the tapping of many knives on plates could be a terrifying experience. It was even known for men to go hungry rather than face such a possibility! In general, students were told to "work hard, play hard and pray hard," and the Principal saw to it that, as far as was in his power, they did all these. Many a man not playing a game was obliged to accompany the Principal for an afternoon walk if caught loitering in the corridors. Organised games and sport flourished, and the College held an honourable place in inter-college and university fixtures. The Association football Shield was secured in the 1933-4 season with the loss of only one point (a draw with Richmond College), the Tennis Shield was won for four years running between 1932 and 1936, and the Cricket Shield in 1935. But these are only examples of successes similarly achieved on many other occasions.

Of this period, one former student has written:

"In some ways the College gave the impression of being a highly organised machine, where young men could obtain their qualifications for entering the Ministry, provided that they didn't weaken. It did, however, allow men room to develop their own distinctive gifts. So the College produced academic scholars; indeed, they were encouraged. It also produced its pastors, its missionaries, its administrators, its conservative and liberal Churchmen. Most of the students exhibited in their ministries a pastoral zeal and a seriousness about their vocation with an evangelistic aim which was, perhaps, the best that the College could give. Provided a man conformed to the discipline (and it was rigid), he could lay a good foundation for his subsequent ministry, but whether he did so or not depended largely on his own initiative and enterprise. He might not be inspired to gain a faith, but the faith he possessed would be sorely tested this way and that by the critical nature of the lectures that he attended. If he stood firm, and was able to reshape his beliefs during those years, the probability was that he would stand firm in the faith for life. The old 'Highbury' was a shaking experience, from which a man could emerge by the grace of God, stronger intellectually and spiritually than when he had entered."

The large increase in the number of students enabled fees to be kept at a minimum, which was an important consideration when many men were in receipt of grants. In fact, the College finances, skilfully managed by the Principal, enabled a considerable sum to be invested towards increasing the endowments.

79

Relations with London University were again causing some concern at this time, particularly with regard to the representation of the teaching staff on the governing body of the Hall. The University authorities were pressing for the teaching staff to elect a member to represent them on the Council, but the Council objected on the ground that many differences existed between St. John's Hall and the other constituent colleges of the University. The Hall was controlled by a scheme which specifically provided for the government of the College, and the Council's memorandum continued:

> "At the present the greatest harmony prevails, and the Principal is consulted on every matter of importance. But if and when it becomes necessary to secure some revision of the scheme, this matter will again be most carefully and impartially considered with other matters calling for amendment of the Scheme."

And there for the time being the matter rested.

Among changes on the Council and staff at this period were the elections of the Rev. J. M. Hewitt, Vicar of Islington, and Mr. H. B. Barkworth in 1933, while the Rev. Martin Parsons resigned from the staff at the end of 1934 to work for the Church Mission to Jews in Poland. The Rev. T. C. Hammond was appointed tutor in 1935. An LL.B. of Trinity College, Dublin, he had obtained a first class Theological Exhibition, and came to Highbury after a three-year curacy at St. Jude's, Belfast.

But the most important concern of the College authorities from 1932 to 1935 was the initiation of steps towards the granting of a diploma, with the right to carry the designation "Associate of the London College of Divinity." A scheme was drawn up which included the following points:

A. 1. Students must take the three-year post-matriculation course and pass all examinations.

2. Students taking B.D. must take extra subjects as arranged by the Principal, such subjects being those required for the General Ordination Examination.

3. Graduates may qualify by taking a two-year course.

4. Men already ordained might qualify by taking a two-year course.

5. In all cases, students must take the whole of the subjects of the prescribed course, including Latin and Greek.

6. Older non-graduates sent by bishops for a special two-year course were not eligible.

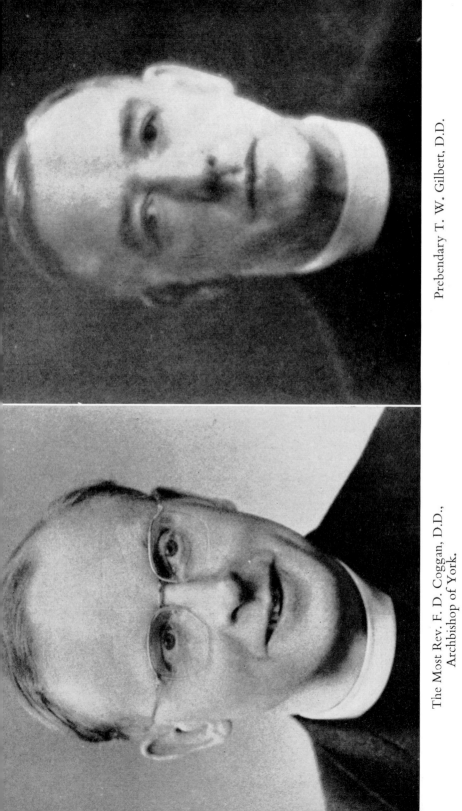

The Most Rev. F. D. Coggan, D.D.,
Archbishop of York.

Prebendary T. W. Gilbert, D.D.

The Present Principal, the Rev. Hugh Jordan, B.D.

Interior of Chapel.

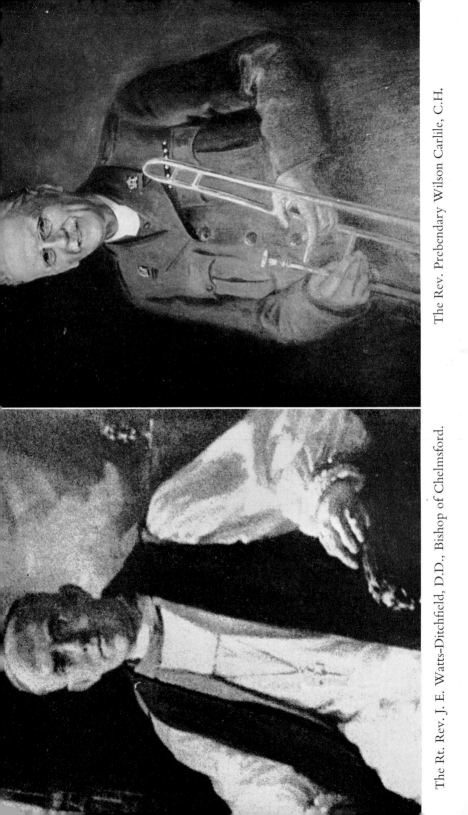

The Rt. Rev. J. E. Watts-Ditchfield, D.D., Bishop of Chelmsford.

The Rev. Prebendary Wilson Carlile, C.H.

The Most Rev. Hugh Gough, D.D.,
Archbishop of Sydney.

The Most Rev. L. W. Brown, D.D.,
Archbishop of Uganda.

The Rt. Rev. John Taylor Smith,
K.C.B., C.V.O., D.D.,
Bishop of Sierra Leone and
Chaplain-General to the Forces.

B and *C*. These sections concerned the new hood, which would be
submitted to the Archbishop for sanction.

D. Though students should pass the necessary examinations, they
must also be formally "elected" as associates by the Council,
which would appear on the diploma. Honorary associates
might also, though seldom, be elected.

E. The scheme of College work, under which the A.L.C.D. would
be granted, was recognised by C.A.C.T.M. in 1923, but the
associateship would only date from 1928.

F. The A.L.C.D. hood would be rigidly restricted to those who
fulfilled A.L.C.D. requirements. The existing College hood
could still be used by those who had two years' residence, and
had passed the two-year course.

G. The A.L.C.D. could not be made public until the formal
approval of the bishops had been secured.

C.A.C.T.M.'s approval for this scheme was unanimously given on
March 21st, 1934, and the way was now open to proceed with plans
for making this a great occasion. Despite certain opposition on the
Council, the Archbishop of Canterbury, Dr. Lang, was invited to give
the first diplomas. The date was fixed for June 27th, 1935, when a
distinguished company gathered in the Merchant Taylors' hall. The
procession included members of the College staff and Council, the
Principal, the Archdeacon of London, Canon S. L. Brown, D.D., the
Bishops of Barking and Stepney (Curzon), and the Archbishop of
Canterbury. Proceedings began with the singing unaccompanied of
the 100th Psalm. There followed a Bidding Prayer, beautifully composed and read by Dr. Harold Smith. The Bishop of Barking, as
President of the Council, then paid tribute to the College founders,
Alfred and Kezia Peache, and to the four Principals. Dr. Gilbert, who
was greeted with prolonged applause, then rose to explain the history
and significance of the Associateship. It began with negotiations with
King's College, which were approved by C.A.C.T.M. in 1923.

"In effect it means," he continued, "that the syllabus of the General Ordination Examination is practically covered in the first two years of the post-
matriculation course, while the third-year work is on a higher level, being
taken from the London B.D. syllabus for the current year. The Examining
Committee of C.A.C.T.M. appoints external examiners each year. . . .
As far as possible, therefore, King's College and our own College are working
on parallel lines, and are having their work reported on by the same examiner
appointed by C.A.C.T.M."

Dr. Gilbert went on to point out that such a scheme obviously produced a desire for St. John's to receive a diploma similar to the A.K.C., and he expressed sincere gratitude to Prebendary Richard Hanson, then Principal of King's College, for his support in the undertaking. He also thanked the Archbishop of Canterbury and the College Visitor, the Bishop of London, for their help and interest. He concluded:

> "It may be permitted to say that my colleagues on the tutorial staff, to whom the College owes so much for their thorough and scholarly work, are deeply conscious with myself that the granting of the Associateship gives the hall-mark of official recognition to a standard of work of which we are justly proud."

The Archbishop then made a notable speech, first congratulating all concerned in his usual felicitous terms. On the new hood ("that ornament, by many so highly prized,") he pronounced:

> "So far as I am a judge of academic millinery, I see no reason to disapprove of it. However, those who are to receive the title for the first time will wear it for all time upon their backs for the edification of the faithful—an insignia of those who have achieved proficiency in sacred learning."

He addressed his concluding remarks in more serious vein to the past and present students of the College. He reminded them that the first essential was the reality of their own spiritual experience:

> "Without that you have neither any right to believe that you are called by God to this Ministry, nor will you have any prospect of being able to discharge it for the good of man, unless (I may remind you of the characteristically emphatic words of St. Paul) you have been 'put in trust with the Gospel.' I cannot imagine," he went on, "any greater and more responsible office among one's fellow-men than to be the responsible trustees for the proclamation of God's scheme for saving the world. It is obviously impossible to fulfil that trust unless this gospel is to you yourself good news—the best thing that you have, the one thing with which you could not part, so that when you proclaim it to others you are testifying—testifying to that which you have seen and do know."

He then proceeded to emphasise the need for this primary experience to be supplemented by continual reading and study, otherwise that experience might wear thin or become narrow, or, worst of all, become a kind of second-hand convention. There was a great danger that clergymen should utter phrases from year to year until they appeared to be making mere conventional remarks. This could be avoided by study. This did not mean "picking up and reading little books of theology—little pills of theology for easy consumption," but rather study of the great books. These were first and foremost the Scriptures, but also, he urged, "I beg of you always to keep some really good book on hand on which you can stretch, enlarge, enrich your minds." As an illustration, he spoke of an old Highland stalker in a remote cottage who told how he was often snowed up in the winter months, and spent his time reading. The Archbishop offered to send him some magazines and reviews, but was coldly thanked with the words: "I'll no' be fashing wi' trash of that kind!" On being pressed to state what he would like, he said: "If you could only get me Jonathan Edwards on *The Scheme of Salvation*, how I would 'wrastle' with it on the winter nights." Dr. Lang went on to commend books that could be wrestled with, for only books such as these made a real impression upon men. Next he made the significant comment that he spent most of his time trying to awaken the clergy to the need for a living evangelism as an integral part of their ministry, but he added:

"In so many places, the clergy seem to have given up even the expectation that they should be able to do the one thing which they were appointed to do; in the old language, 'to win souls for Christ.'"

He concluded by quoting words of Archbishop Frederick Temple, who said, when speaking of his boys at Rugby, "I will not teach my boys out of stagnant water," and urging his audience to receive their diploma "not merely as a gratifying proof that you have mastered the elements of sacred learning, but as a very solemn pledge that you will continue your pursuit of it to your life's end."

The actual conferring of the Associateships followed. The President performed the "hooding," and the Archbishop handed to each candidate the diploma. When all were seated, Prebendary Hinde, Principal of Oak Hill College and Secretary of the Council, thanked the Archbishop on behalf of the College, and this was seconded by Mr. Albert Mitchell, after which the Archbishop gave the blessing.

These proceedings not only concluded a memorable day, but also marked the fulfilment of many years of hope and effort. It was indeed the most significant event to date in the history of the College, bringing an outward and visible sign of maturity and of the official recognition accorded to the London College of Divinity, together with a mark of confidence placed in its Principal, teachers and teaching in the judgment of the whole Church. In recognition of this great achievement, for which he had worked so long, Dr. Gilbert was presented with an illuminated testimonial, signed by all his senior and deputy senior students, with a large interlocking glass-fronted bookcase, and with a walnut tea table and leather armchair.

Later in 1935, the Council moved some way towards meeting the objections raised by London University. The authorities there had always disliked the omission of any elected representative of the staff on the governing body. The Council therefore resolved that the Principal should henceforth attend all meetings as of right (hitherto he had only been present by invitation) until a vacancy on the Council occurred, upon which he would be elected to that body; and it was further decided "that the Council regard sympathetically the principle that the teaching staff shall, under the control of the Council and in concert with, and under the general leadership of, the Principal, have due part in the management of the scholastic work of the College, and they have always acted on that principle and will continue to do so." This at least secured that a member of the teaching staff, even if not elected by them, had a seat on the governing body.

The year 1936 brought great loss to the College through the sudden death of the Rev. Dr. Harold Smith, after an association of exactly thirty years with St. John's Hall. Of him a former staff member has written:

> "He was the most erudite, and also the best loved member of the staff. Eccentric, careless in dress, often forgetful, relishing a good story, at which he would laugh his characteristic loud laugh, he was a figure recalling a past age of dons. His lectures on Christian morals gave him the opportunity of expressing his pet opinions—one was that the death penalty should be extended to include such offences as blackmail. It was related of him that at the time of the Irish troubles, he would walk up and down the corridor saying to himself, 'Stand them up against the wall and shoot them!' One of the bequests in his will was to the Southern Irish Loyalists' Relief Association."

He belonged to an old Essex family, his father being for over sixty years Churchwarden of Havering-atte-Bower. He was something of a martinet, and during the General Strike of 1926 he sent word that if there was trouble in London, Harold must return home at once! Harold once observed, in a tone of complaint, that when he went home for the vacation, he was packed off to bed early by his nonagenarian parents. He was broader in outlook that most others on the staff, and in conversation would defend the Eastward Position at the Holy Communion. To quote the previous writer once more:

"His lectures were marred by inaudibility (he suffered from deafness, and a rather lisping speech), and students would often complain of the difficulty of 'getting Squiffy down.' In later years his lecture notes were duplicated, but though this improved matters to some extent, his inaudible asides when amplifying the written material, often accompanied by laughing at his own jokes, were hardly conducive to order, and a certain amount of ragging took place. A very humble-minded man, he opened the treasures of his knowledge freely."

It was a misfortune for the Church that his physical disabilities would have prevented his accepting higher office, for which his intellectual gifts eminently fitted him. In addition to his *Ante-Nicene Exegesis of the Gospels*, six volumes, published by S.P.C.K., his other main work was *The Ecclesiastical History of Essex under the Long Parliament and the Commonweatlh*, which was published in 1932.

A tablet to his memory was unveiled in the College chapel by the President, the Bishop of Barking, on February 18th, 1937.

In 1936 the Rev. E. G. Bevan left to become Vicar of St. Paul's, Leyton. The Council expressed their deep appreciation of his services to the College during the eleven years that he had been on the staff. He was succeeded by the Rev. S. G. Steer as Vice-Principal and Bursar; he also held the post of Chaplain to the Mercers' Company. Mr. D. W. C. Ford, the former Senior Student, became assistant tutor. At the same time the Rev. W. G. Brown, B.D., after a short period on the staff, left for the mission field in India. In 1938 the Rev. T. C. Hammond left to become Vicar of St. Luke's, Manningham, Bradford, and the Rev. J. W. Wenham, who had obtained a second class in the Theological Tripos at Cambridge, was appointed tutor. In 1939 Mr. D. G. Sherriff, a London B.D. and former student, joined the staff as student lecturer. On the Council, the resignations took place of Mr. Buxton in 1938 and of Commander Studd the following year. An arrangement which came to an end in 1939 concerned the St. Catherine's Deaconness House, Highbury. It began in 1924, at a time when an overall system for deaconness's training had not been fully settled. A two-year course in theology was required, and a number of women students came to St. John's Hall for the lectures attended by those men taking the General Ordination Examination, with the exception that the women did no Greek. Deaconness Warman was for much of the time in charge, and the arrangement was facilitated with the help of her brother, Bishop Guy Warman of Manchester. Twenty-one women in all took the course, of whom eleven were ordained, most of the rest becoming full-time parish workers. Dr. Gilbert took a great interest in this work, and assisted in one of the ordination services at St. Paul's Cathedral.

The years 1937 to 1939 were overshadowed by the threat of war. Though the number of students declined slightly, it still remained over ninety. The Principal, who was formally elected to the Council in March, 1939, was instructed to make arrangements for evacuation in the event of hostilities commencing, and at first agreement was reached to go to Oak Hill College at Southgate, whose Principal was Prebendary Hinde, Secretary to the St. John's Hall Council.

On the outbreak of war, Dr. Gilbert decided to divide the College; thirty-eight men went to Oak Hill and thirty-seven remained at Highbury. There were, of course, many anxieties and restrictions. For some time there was suspense as to the call-up of men for service in the Forces. Fire-watching, first aid and air raid precaution duties had to be organised, and the Thursday evening Chapel service was discontinued. In November, 1940, the College was severely damaged by a parachute mine, during a raid in which Cox, the College gardener, was killed. Roofs, ceilings and window-frames were so affected as to make the buildings unusable. The men, now fifty-six in all, were therefore evacuated, two of the houses at Wadhurst School for Girls, near Tunbridge Wells, being placed at the disposal of the College. Here St. John's found a temporary home, the parish church being used as a College chapel. The expenses of removal to Wadhurst were considerable, and with the decreasing income from students' fees, finances became somewhat strained. Despite increasing difficulties, however, Mrs. Gilbert and the domestic staff coped nobly with food and fuel rationing, and work was carried on as far as possible. The number of students dropped from an average of eighty-eight in 1939, to sixty-six in 1940, fifty-six in 1941, and twenty-six in 1942, as war service caused an increasing number of prospective candidates to defer their training for ordination.

Two members of the Council who had given long service to the College died during 1941, Messrs. J. F. W. Deacon and W. G. Bradshaw. The latter had been a member for thirty-five years, and Treasurer for eighteen, "which onerous duties", in the opinion of the Council, "he discharged with marked success." They paid tribute to his care and diligence, particularly in connection with the lengthy negotiations which he had conducted regarding the sale of the College property to the Arsenal Football Club. Mr. W. G. Spooner was elected a Council member in his place. At the end of 1940, the Principal received congratulation on being appointed Dean of the Faculty of Theology in London University, a well-merited tribute to his scholarship and teaching ability. Just over a year later, all present and past students were delighted to learn that the Bishop of London, Dr. Fisher, had appointed Dr. Gilbert a Prebendary of St. Paul's. He was also nominated as representative on the Collegiate Council of London University.

The question of the College buildings was giving some cause for concern. In March, 1941, the Council agreed to the letting of the basement for a stretcher-party depot, and in June, 1942, the Principal was reporting that the whole College would be requisitioned by the National Fire Service, which in fact took place at the end of the month. But at this time yet further misfortune struck the College in the sudden death of Dr. Gilbert at Wadhurst. He had suffered from illness, and though making a good recovery, he returned to work too soon, and died on June 22nd. In their resolution expressing profound sorrow at the grievous loss which they had sustained, the Council declared that Dr. Gilbert had—

"discharged the responsibilities inherent in his office in a way which has won, and throughout maintained, both the confidence of the Council and the affectionate loyalty of the students, as well as the esteem of the Church and the respect of the University."

In 1926, at a time of great perplexity, he had been appointed executive head of its affairs, and he had raised the College to a position where it had never been stronger nor more effective. They thanked God for the gift of His servant, and extended to Mrs. Gilbert, who had so ably assisted him, and to his daughter their heartfelt sympathy.

Tributes to Dr. Gilbert's life and work came in from near and far. In so many ways he earned the respect and affection of those who worked with him and under him. He was an intensely hard worker, and never spared himself. Many of his afternoons were spent visiting the district around from door to door to find lodgings for his students. Always decided in his views on important matters, and prepared to defend them with good reasons, he was never intolerant of the opinions of others. He could be very angry and show it, but his anger was short-lived and under perfect control. The Rev. E. G. Bevan relates this story:

"One of his old choirboys in Oxford told me recently of a saying current among themselves: 'When Tommy puts his glasses on, something's going to shift!'"

Old Johnians will understand and appreciate this! He knew his students better than many of them imagined, for he was not naturally approachable, but those who confided in him found a real friend and helper. His somewhat forbidding exterior was partly due to shyness, which men did not realise until they came into close touch with him. But letters from former students make clear that those who penetrated beneath the surface found an immense fund of wisdom, experience, and hard common sense placed at their disposal. Such phrases as "I owe more to you and to the time spent at Highbury and to what God did for me there than anyone will ever know" are common. Another wrote: "I have no compunction in saying to myself when faced with the need of putting some of your advice into practice, 'The Principal tried it and it worked, so try it!'" One very shy student twice went to the Principal's study on his first day and begged to be allowed to leave. He was treated with great gentleness and persuaded to try and stay for a few days. By half-term, he so loved the place that he did not even go away for the "open" week-end! Others will recall Dr. Gilbert's policy of unbending gradually. To first-year men he seemed aloof. In their second year, men found him in his advisory capacity, but in the third year he became a friend. Again, who will forget his lectures in dogmatic theology which we vainly tried to get down in longhand; or the twinkle behind the gold-rimmed spectacles when he described his own lectures on the Doctrine of God as "exhaustive and exhausting"! He taught that perspiration and inspiration were not to be confused, though both were necessary in a successful student.

He did not lack critics; it was said that the College was isolated from the main stream of Anglican life, as witnessed by the fact that preachers in the College chapel, bishops excepted, were only those clergymen who were familiar figures on Evangelical platforms; and that the type of piety which prevailed in the college tended to be more emotional than intellectual, "fostered by the sentimentalism of many of the hymns in 'Lady Carbery's Hymn Book.'" But the same critic hastens to add:

"No man had his head less in the clouds and his feet more firmly on the ground than the Principal, and in the one serious difference between us, I now own that I was in the wrong."

An extract from an appreciation paid by the Council's President in *The Times* must conclude this endeavour to convey the gratitude and respect of all who knew him for Dr. Gilbert's great services to St. John's:

"He was an admirable organiser and administrator, and he leaves the finances of the college in a sound position. . . . Many of his friends expected that he would be appointed to the charge of a home diocese, but his sixteen years at Highbury were perhaps as useful service as any man could render to the Church."[1]

[1] *The Times*, June 26th, 1942.

CHAPTER V

Calamity and Resurgence, 1942-63

THE calamity of war had, by midsummer, 1942, reduced a thriving College to a mere building shell, occupied after requisitioning by the National Fire Service; a College which had also suffered the loss of its energetic and deeply respected Principal, and whose students, now a mere handful in number, were maintaining a precarious existence after evacuation to a school in Sussex. Three courses were now open to those whose training for the Ministry was still the College's responsibility:

  i. That they should continue at Wadhurst.
 ii. That they should be transferred to Bristol to share lectures with King's College.
iii. That they should co-exist with Oak Hill College at Southgate.

After much discussion by the Council, the third course was adopted, and the Principal, Prebendary Hinde, was appointed also acting Principal of St. John's, with power to engage the necessary staff. The Vice-Principal, the Rev. S. C. Steer had left to return to Canada, as Principal of Emmanuel College, Saskatoon; and the Rev. J. W. Wenham had gone to St. Matthew's, Cambridge, as curate, both in the summer of 1941. Arrangements were therefore made to terminate the position at Wadhurst, and the appointment of a new Principal was deferred.

Another matter before the Council, which had been under discussion for some time, was the inauguration of a board of patronage. It was decided in July, 1942, that this should be set up, and advowsons accepted, but the Trust would not be under obligation to confine their nominees to former St. John's students, though, if available, they would receive careful consideration. The Trust's principles would be definitely Evangelical and Protestant, based upon Scripture as the sole rule of faith, and the only true foundation of a ministry of the gospel of the grace of God. It was decided that, while trustees would generally be Council members, this need not necessarily be the case.

The position of the College academically was not discouraging at the end of 1942. Eight men had taken B.D. during the year, and two the M.Th., while thirteen had qualified for the A.L.C.D., a fair enough record in the circumstances. Early in 1943, changes took place on the Council. Canon H. F. S. Adams resigned through ill-health, and was thanked for his services over the previous nineteen years. New members who joined were Canon St. John Thorpe, Vicar of Watford, the Rev. H. Earnshaw Smith, Vicar of All Souls', Langham Place, and Mr. Frank Kidner. Discussion now took place as to the future of the College, and a committee of three, consisting of the President and the Revs. Dr. F. Bate and J. M. Hewitt, was set up to confer with a similar committee from Oak Hill College as to the practicability of keeping St. John's "in being" at Oak Hill. As to a new Principal, it was decided to enquire whether the Rev. F. D. Coggan, then Professor of New Testament at Wycliffe College, Toronto, who had formerly been curate to Mr. Hewitt at Islington Parish Church, would consider the post. As Mr. Coggan was conducting clergy schools throughout Canada during the long vacation, he asked leave to postpone his decision until the late summer. By September, however, he sent a cable accepting the position, which was unanimously confirmed to date from August 1st, 1944.

Mr. Coggan had had a notable academic career at Cambridge. A scholar of St. John's College, Cambridge, he had gained a first class in both parts of the Oriental Languages Tripos, the Jeremie Septuagint and Mason Hebrew prizes, and Tyrwhitt Hebrew Scholarship, and was Naden Divinity student. After a lectureship in Semitic languages and literatures at Manchester University, he was ordained in 1934 to a curacy at St. Mary, Islington, leaving for Toronto in 1937 to become Professor of New Testament at Wycliffe College, which awarded him their Doctorate of Divinity *honoris causa* when he returned to England. It was in May, 1944, that he zigzagged across the north Atlantic in a banana boat to take up his new assignment, and travelled by train overnight from Stranraer to London. Here he found evidence of Hitler's attentions both to the city and College. The old buildings which he had known in his Islington days bore many honourable scars, and presented a desolate and forlorn appearance. The only human link with the College of former days was the porter, Samuel Fuzzard, who gripped his hand and said: "I'll stand by you, sir"—a promise amply fulfilled in the succeeding years. Despite Fuzzard's vigilance, the theft had occurred of various articles, such as curtains and blankets, and the outlook was grim and bleak.

Dr. Coggan began the Michaelmas Term at Oak Hill with three men. The shadow of Dr. Boultbee and the opening months of his Principalship may well have haunted the place! It was clear that some long-term planning was a matter of urgency, and a committee was therefore set up to consider the future location of the College. It consisted of the Principal, the Rev. T. G. Mohan, and Messrs. Keith, Kidner and Mitchell. They met seven times in the course of the year June, 1944, to June, 1945, and, since their recommendations vitally affected the future history of the College, their discussions must be considered in some detail. They first met on June 28th, 1944, at C.M.S. House, Salisbury Square, some three weeks after "D-Day," when the possibility of the war being over by the end of the year was in the minds of some. If this were the case, plans must be drawn up as rapidly as possible to allow for a speedy intake of men demobilised from the Forces. But the overriding consideration was the matter of locality. Three possibilities were considered:

i. To remain at Highbury. It was reasonably near the University and in the London diocese. It had a fine chapel and dining-hall; but as against this, the neighbourhood had declined badly, and was not likely to recover. Also the buildings in parts were dark and gloomy, and only partially centrally heated.

ii. To build anew. This would be the ideal course, but it would be costly. The money in hand, though substantial, would not cover the expense, and would have to be augmented from elsewhere.

iii. To buy a house to be adapted and extended, and various firms had been approached to look into the matter.

The committee decided to keep in touch with London University, and to remain within the London Diocese. While an entirely new building would be preferable, its cost was adjudged to be prohibitive, and it seemed probable that they would have to stay on at Highbury for some years. On reporting to the Council, consultations on the matter took place with individuals and with various firms, in the course of which the third possibility was held to be impracticable. On the other hand, contrary to views previously expressed, it was discovered that to purchase a site and build a new college might not be as costly as was at first estimated. At their September meeting, tentative plans were put forward for a new building on a site at Brockley Hill, near Edgware. There was still a strong feeling among some Council members that the old Highbury site should be retained, but after one member, who was also on the Council, had visited the site and reported on the deplorable state of the buildings and of the neighbourhood, the committee passed a unanimous resolution that it was in the best interests of the College to move, and in their opinion Brockley Hill was the best site then available. This was endorsed on a majority vote by the Council the same month.

By the beginning of 1945, the Principal could state to the committee that a lot of work had been done. Further properties had been inspected at Elstree, Wrotham, Stanmore and Northwood, and the last seemed to be the most suitable. It was first suggested by the Rev. J. G. Downward, of Emmanuel Church, Northwood, and his curate the Rev. F. H. C. Gray, an Old Johnian. The site had been visited by Mr. W. C. Waymouth, F.R.I.B.A., and by Dr. Coggan, and both had inspected an adjoining house, which would be suitable for a Principal's residence. The situation was good; the area known as Broad Oak Field, consisting of seven acres, was by itself too small, but the adjacent property of "Wetherby", with three and a half acres becoming available shortly afterwards, gave double the frontage, with room for a games field. The committee decided to recommend to the Council that the whole site, comprising ten and a half acres, including "Wetherby," should be purchased, providing—

(a) The local Borough Council agreed to a college being built in that area.

(b) Questions of drainage and soil were satisfactory.

(c) That the executors of "Wetherby" would sell it and its grounds.

It was decided that an appeal for funds should be made to the Evangelical public. In February, the Council passed a resolution expressing a favourable impression of "Wetherby" and the adjoining property, but as such a scheme was a large and comprehensive one, it was felt that the Council could not be committed immediately to purchase without further careful and exhaustive enquiries, and an extension of time was therefore essential. The report of Mr. Waymouth on the property was favourable, and the estimated cost did not appear unreasonable.

In March, 1945, Prebendary Hinde resigned as Secretary to the

College Council, having occupied that position for eighteen years. The President expressed warm thanks for his services and the Council's regret at his resignation, at the same time handing him a cheque in recognition of their gratitude. He was succeeded as Secretary by the Rev. T. G. Mohan, and Mr. A. B. Keith was appointed Treasurer. Congratulations were extended to the Principal on his appointment as a recognised teacher of the University, and on taking his place as a member of the Board of Studies in Theology. The Council also felt it advisable that the Principal should inform the authorities of the Arsenal Football Club as to the possibility of a move, and that Old Johnians should be given some preliminary information as to future plans.

Meanwhile, the position of the handful of students during 1944-5, carrying on at Oak Hill College, was not easy. They were some eight or nine in all, but numbers in the College were made up by some C.M.S. missionary recruits. It was also difficult for the two Principals to have to live and work together so closely with their small student body. But one there at this time has written:

> "Prebendary Hinde won the respect of us all, for he was a man of iron will, but with deep devotion to our Lord. That winter of 1944-5 was bitterly cold. We sat in our studies with cassocks (and oftentimes dressing-gowns) on, and tried to study with the temperature well below freezing; the austerity of war made central heating in the building impossible. Those were the days when there were no C.A.C.T.M. grants, and fees at the College were £90 per annum. In the grim autumn of 1944, we watched from the terrace in front of the College the flying bombs passing over London. The following year, the Principal, now joined by Mrs. Coggan and their two children from Toronto, had to work with a new Principal of Oak Hill, the Rev. L. F. E. Wilkinson. This we felt was a happy combination, since the intellectual stimulus of Dr. Coggan's lectures was balanced by the practical insights of the lectures of the Principal of Oak Hill. One of the least formal memories of both these years and one of the happiest, were the hours we spent in Dr. Coggan's drawing-room on a Sunday evening. After coffee and sandwiches, and talk, we would sing hymns (for which Dr. Coggan would play the piano), and close with prayer. For many of us it was a touch of home away from home."

In June, 1945, College fees were raised from £90 to £110 per annum. The College staff was augmented by the appointments of a Vice-Principal and tutor, the Revs. F. W. Dillistone and R. S. Dean. The former had gained a scholarship to Brasenose College, Oxford, where he took a first class in Mathematical Moderations. He took his

Oxford B.D. in 1933, was awarded an honorary D.D. of Toronto University in 1946, and gained an Oxford D.D. in 1951 for his thesis on "The Structure of the Divine Society." Mr. Dean, a former Senior Student, took his London B.D. in 1938, and the M.Th. in 1944. The acquisition of two scholars of this calibre was a great asset to the College.

The ending of the war in the summer of 1945 made possible a greater concentration of planning upon future developments. The College had played its part in that forty Old Johnians served as Army chaplains and nine as chaplains to the Royal Air Force. The September reunion gathering was held at St. Dunstan in the West, Fleet Street, and St. Andrew's Hall, Holborn, lent by an Old Johnian, the Rev. J. Russell Howden. Some fifty were present, and were addressed by the Principal on the future of the College.

One of the many problems facing Dr. Coggan at this time was the condition of the library at St. John's Hall. His visit in the summer of 1944 was not reassuring. The entire floor was covered with furniture and bedding gathered from all parts of the blitzed College, rising in huge stacks some eight feet high. Around the central pile was a narrow way by which the visitor might look through the door of the book-cases, which could not always be opened, owing to the confined space. But on the shelves themselves all semblance of order had disappeared: one volume of a series might be at one end of the library and the next volume at the other end. As for the shelves, firewood being scarce, some had been ripped out and burnt, while part of the roof had been blown off by bomb damage. The weather being unkind, mildew grew apace on some book-covers. But this was as nothing compared to the tragedy of two years later. From a cause officially unknown, but generally suspected to have been a visit by a gang of small boys, a fire broke out in the old west wing on the night of May 7th, 1946, which completely took off the library roof, gutted much of the Principal's house and of "the Cockpit," and damaged the west tower. Several thousands of books were saved, but many of the oldest and most valuable were destroyed or reduced to charred pulp by fire and water. Fortunately, the furniture, which, until recently had been stored in the library, had been moved to another part of the College, and was unaffected. Though some £6,000 was paid by the insurance company in settlement of the claim, it would be true to say that, at least so far as the old and rare books are concerned, the College library has never fully recovered from this disaster. But for those waverers who still retained longings for the old Highbury site, this further damage made any idea of a return unthinkable.

Meanwhile, in the autumn of 1945 the Bishop of Barking tendered his resignation after twenty-one years as President of the College Council—years which had seen the appointment of two Principals, the granting of the Associateship, and the complete dislocation of the College life and work owing to world war. The Council expressed their "deep sense of gratitude" and "their appreciation of his untiring labours for the welfare of the College." It was Bishop Inskip who had conducted negotiations with the Board of Education as to the College's status; with London University over stabilising relations between it and the College; and with C.A.C.T.M. and with individual bishops on many matters. The College were indeed fortunate to have had the privilege of his devoted service during such a significant period of its history. He was appointed a Vice-President, as was Bishop Gwynne at this time. His successor as President was the Bishop of Sodor and Man (the Rt. Rev. J. R. S. Taylor, D.D.), formerly Principal of Wycliffe Hall, Oxford, who, having had more than ten years' first-hand experience in charge of a theological college, was fully able to appreciate the many problems with which St. John's was now confronted. At the end of 1945, the Council surrendered the lease of St. John's Hall buildings to the Arsenal Football Club, subject to special arrangements made for compensation. So terminated an association with Highbury which had lasted for almost eighty years; but with a natural feeling of sadness there went an accompanying hopeful anticipation. When so many were making new beginnings in life and service, St. John's would at least be in good company.

The new year began with the appointment as architect of Mr. R. Fielding Dodd, F.R.I.B.A. He had already done important work at Stowe School, at St. Peter's Hall, Oxford, and also at Wycliffe Hall. He was given three main directives:

(a) That the College buildings should be worthy of the Evangelical principles for which it has always stood.
(b) That it should centre around the chapel, which might in some way be linked with the library.
(c) That it should accommodate seventy-five students, each having separate bedroom and study on the same floor, together with rooms for the Vice-Principal and one married tutor, Senior and Junior Common Rooms, four lecture-rooms and a guest-room.

These directives had subsequently to be modified, as will be seen. The chapel should be large enough to seat 100 students, with additional accommodation for visitors, and should be built in the classical rather than the Gothic style. It was clear that, despite funds in hand, a large sum of additional money would be needed to complete the project, and plans went forward for launching a public appeal.

But the most pressing question was that of accommodation, since the premises at Oak Hill were becoming too congested for both colleges. The Rev. T. W. Graham, formerly Rector of Weymouth, had been requested to try to find suitable quarters, and in March, 1946, he brought before the Council "West Acre," one of the School houses at Harrow. This was taken on a two-year lease, though in fact the College only stayed for one year, and here St. John's really recovered its individuality. In the summer the Principal could report:[1]

> "If you could pay us a visit . . . you would find us happily installed at West Acre . . . a full-time staff of four, the Revs. F. W. Dillistone, R. S. Dean, R. G. G. Hooper and myself, together with a part-time lecturer, the Rev. Geoffrey Parke-Taylor. I must not fail also to mention our Lady House-keeper, Miss Elizabeth Churchill, who has done wonders in making us feel at home in new surroundings, and Fuzzard, known for many years to our Johnian family. Our numbers stand at forty-eight, twenty-five of these being new this year. Most are ex-Service men, and bring to their preparation for the Ministry a real experience of life, and I am thankful to add, of God."

The Rev. R. G. G. Hooper was an old Johnian, and senior student in 1941-2. A London B.D., he subsequently obtained a second class in the Theological Tripos at Cambridge, and came back to his old College, after two years as tutor at Oak Hill, to serve as tutor and chaplain until his return to parochial work in 1952. Other matters raised at this time included the reappointment of the Rev. Professor Sydney Cave, D.D., to serve as the theological colleges' representative on the Collegiate Council of London University. A deepened sense of unity in common endeavour arose through the holding of another reunion in September. There had been a special gathering to welcome the new Principal in September, 1944, at Sion College, and a meeting in September, 1945, but this was a more ambitious affair. After a lapse during the war years, it was the more deeply appreciated by the twenty-eight members who enjoyed the fellowship and hospitality at "West Acre," while thirty-four others joined on the second day. Those taking part were the President of the Old Johnians' Association, the Rev. T. Ashton,

[1] *Johnian*, Michaelmas Term, 1946.

Prebendary E. A. Dunn and the Principal, who preached the sermon at Christ Church, Roxeth. Two papers were read on "Proclaiming the Gospel in the Post-war World" by the Rev. D. K. Dean and the Ven. F. E. Wilcock, Archdeacon of Onitsha in the Diocese of the Niger, while the closing address was given by the Rev. E. G. A. Dunn. This proved a most happy and helpful gathering, leading not unnaturally to a desire for a return to the pre-war practice of a full-scale residential reunion as soon as possible.

It was agreed that the College should be affiliated with the School of English Church Music, and a notable visitor during the Lent Term, 1947, was Sir Sidney Nicholson, Principal of the Royal School of Church Music and formerly organist of Westminster Abbey. He gave two lectures on the theme, "What the Church Musician asks from the Clergy," and pleaded for intelligent interest in the work of the choir and in church music generally, with practical advice on the training of choirs, choice of hymns and tunes and pointing of psalms. His visit stimulated much interest, and gave to many a new insight into the place of music in Christian worship. In the College very happy relations existed with the Vicar (J. N. Hoare) and Parish of Christ Church, Roxeth, where the College services were conducted, and with Harrow School, whose Headmaster, the late R. W. Moore, showed "no little kindness" to this unexpected addition to his "family."

Another sign that matters were returning to normal was the revival of that hardy annual, the "Binge," or, to the uninitiated, the concert which customarily closes the Michaelmas Term. Its origins are wrapped in mystery, but certainly go back some sixty years. Its usual form consists of a few glees, interspersed with sketches, in which each "year" vies with the other two to produce something of a light and diverting character wherein topical incidents are exploited, individual misfortunes exposed, and the eccentricities of the staff are not spared. The presence of a mock lyric-writer among the students is revealed on such occasions with surprising frequency, and the verses composed may be of high quality, often consisting of adaptations of popular B.B.C. programmes or of well-known light entertainment. Indeed, some of the script-writers and actors have manifested such gifts that it has sometimes been suggested that they have missed their vocation. But doubtless the performers have found such talents of great value for parish socials and similar less serious occasions in after years. So the "Binge" continues year by year to add its quota to the old Highbury tradition.

During the autumn of 1946 plans for launching the appeal for the College rebuilding had gone steadily forward. The Rev. R. F. Penfold was appointed appeal organiser, and contacts were made with the Press. Frequent meetings were held of the appeals and buildings committees, and an air of purpose and of hopeful anticipation prevailed. The actual sending out of the appeal was signalled by a letter which appeared in *The Times* of March 13th, 1947, in the following terms:

"Sir,—The Archbishops of Canterbury and York have frequently pointed out in recent months how serious is the decline in the number of clergy within the Church of England, and how urgent is the need of training men to fill the vacant places. In 1914 there were some 22,000 ordained men. Now there are about 13,000. The London College of Divinity (St. John's Hall, Highbury) is the only one of the theological colleges of the Church of England which has been deprived of its buildings by the war. In addition to damage done by bombs, the College suffered much destruction by a serious fire last year.

"During the last eighty-four years, St. John's Hall has trained many hundreds of candidates for the ministry, including men like John Edwin Watts-Ditchfield, Wilson Carlile, C.H., John Taylor Smith and Llewellyn Gwynne. If it is to continue this work it must have new buildings. A site has already been purchased at Northwood and plans have been drawn. The estimated cost of the whole scheme is approximately £200,000, and of this sum about half is in hand. The chapel is to be a memorial to Bishop Taylor Smith. We ask the hospitality of your columns to bring our need before your readers, believing that a gift towards the rebuilding of the College will be a true contribution to the re-establishing of the Christian order in the world.

"Gifts may be sent to, and further information received from, the Rev. R. F. Penfold, Hill House, Firle Road, North Lancing.

"Yours faithfully,

"Ralph Sodor and Man (*President*),
"Caldecote (*Vice-President*),
"J. T. Barking (*Vice-President*),
"F. D. Coggan (*Principal*),
"A. B. Keith (*Treasurer*).
"London College of Divinity."

Once again, the matter of accommodation was becoming urgent, as Harrow School required "West Acre" for their own use. So on a rainy day in the spring of 1947, after one of the worst winters in living memory, Mr. and Mrs. Dean and Mr. Hooper set out from Harrow for Ford Manor, Lingfield, on what was becoming a desperate search. To quote Mr. Dean's own words:

"As we drew near to the manor we hardly dared hope that our visit would be fruitful; it seemed just too good to be true after so many disappointing forays. . . . Well do I remember crawling on hands and knees round a room piled high with furniture and wondering if it had the dimensions for a possible chapel. It had! . . . 'Yes, this would do for the Principal's study (after all, was it not once the X-ray room in a Canadian base hospital?), and surely we could get at least two students in this room!' And so on. Our hopes were rising rapidly. . . . Back to Harrow we went, feeling very much like Joshua and Caleb reporting to Moses concerning the land of Canaan. We must have told a good story for the Principal evinced interest at once and very soon it was decided. . . . We all felt that this move was right and in the line of the will of God for the College at this particular point in its history. And so it proved to be."

Accordingly, in the summer of 1947, a ten-year lease of Ford Manor at Lingfield was drawn up. It was no small thing to transplant a college, always associated with urban conditions, to the quite different atmosphere of rural life, and there were many wonderings and some fears as to the possibility of settling down in such new surroundings. It was a lovely situation, a country mansion approached down a long drive. After full discussion concerning facilities for worship and for practical work for students, together with the relationship of the college to C.A.C.T.M. and to London University, it was decided to take up the lease from the owner, the Hon. Mrs. Spender-Clay, and here the college stayed for exactly ten years. Surroundings were almost palatial compared with the austerities of West Acre and Oak Hill. The chapel was fitted out in excellent taste, some of the seats from the old Highbury chapel being adapted for use by the resourceful Fuzzard. Here were set up the eagle lectern and Bible, now somewhat scarred by the 1946 fire; and also the Holy Table from the old chapel was restored to its original purpose.

Several staff changes took place in 1947. The Vice-Principal, the Rev. Dr. F. W. Dillistone, left to become Professor of Theology in the Episcopal Theological School, Cambridge, Massachusetts. The loss of this eminent scholar was felt most keenly by the whole College. The Council offered him their sincere congratulations on his appointment, and extended their thanks for his work on behalf of St. John's. Dr. Dillistone returned to England as Chancellor of Liverpool Cathedral in 1952, and succeeded Dr. Dwelly as Dean in 1956. The Rev. R. S. Dean became Vice-Principal, and the Rev. Douglas Webster was appointed tutor. He had gained a second class in theology at Oxford, and had served curacies at St. Helens, Lancashire and at Christ Church, Crouch End. Mr. David Brown, Senior Student the previous year, also joined as student lecturer. A first class B.D., he also gained an M.Th., and was appointed to lecture in Greek and Hebrew. Two new Council members elected in 1947 were the Rev. H. R. Gough, Vicar of Islington, and Mr. J. H. Cordle.

The Principal pointed out to the Council that London University were once again raising the question of a representative of the staff being elected to the governing body. After considerable discussion, the President expressed the prevailing view of most members by stating that such representation "was difficult to justify in principle and might have unfortunate results." Meanwhile, pressure of another kind was being exerted from a different quarter. During the autumn of 1947 the authorities of C.A.C.T.M. asked that a Long Vacation term should be introduced. This was an entirely new departure, but it was agreed to as part of the final preparation for third-year men only, and study would be primarily concerned with the devotional life and pastoralia.

A visitation from London University early in 1948 once more brought adverse comment over staff representation, and upon the fact that choice of a Principal was restricted to a graduate of specific universities, excluding London. This appeared highly inappropriate, and the Council undertook to secure the revision of that obsolete restriction, but resolved still to oppose the request regarding staff representation. It was not, in fact, until 1952 that the revised College scheme of government incorporated this and other modifications. Further criticism from the University authorities concerned the inadequacy of the teaching staff, and it was now decided that the numbers should be raised as soon as possible to five full-time graduate members. With regard to university degrees, it was pointed out that fifty-two B.D.'s had been obtained by St. John's men since 1934, and twelve M.Th.'s since the institution of that degree in 1939, despite the dislocation of the war years. The College finances were in a satisfactory state, but in October, 1948, fees were raised from £120 to £150 per annum.

A new departure at the Principal's suggestion, during the spring of 1948, was the holding of a refresher course for Johnian clergy at Ford Manor from April 12th-16th. Over thirty took advantage of this invitation, ranging in "vintage" from 1901 to 1942. Lectures were given by the Principal on the Epistle to the Ephesians, and by the Revs. R. S. Dean, D. W. C. Ford, R. G. G. Hooper and D. Webster. The course was deeply appreciated by all who attended, and besides the spiritual stimulus and fellowship, it served to show that, though far removed in distance from the old Highbury quarters, the same spirit of devotion and dedication still linked together past and present members of the College.

Another custom which was revived in 1948 was the invitation to an overseas clergyman to spend some time at the College each year. The first to be so invited was the Rev. V. T. Kurien, who came from Travancore, South India, on a strong recommendation from an Old Johnian, the Rev. L. W. Brown, Principal of Kerala United Theological Seminary, and now Archbishop of Uganda. He was followed in subsequent years by clergymen from the Southern Sudan, Nigeria, Kenya, Ceylon, Portugal and elsewhere. The Council granted approval in 1955 for such students already in Anglican orders, of African or Oriental descent, who stayed for one year in the College, to be allowed to wear the College hood. This privilege was greatly valued by those concerned. One of these students, M. N. C. O. Scott, from Fourah Bay College, who spent the year 1950-1 at Lingfield, was consecrated in 1961 Bishop of Sierra Leone.

The first Long Vacation Term, as recommended by C.A.C.T.M., was held during the summer of 1948, and proved a most useful time. During the last week-end, the wives of six men were also invited to be present as guests of the College, a gesture which was so much appreciated that the custom has been continued in subsequent years.

An expansion of practical and pastoral work now began with the holding of missions in various centres. The first was at St. Helens, Lancashire, during the first ten days of April, 1949; the missioner was the Rev. G. J. Rogers, the Men's Candidates' Secretary of C.M.S., assisted by all the full-time College staff, and thirty-eight students, reinforced by a further twenty-two candidates from the C.M.S. training colleges at Foxbury and Liskeard Lodge. The mission covered three parishes, and the reports of the various teams indicated it to have been such a valuable experience that it was decided to arrange others at least once during the course of every student. In the Principal's view, the experiment had been abundantly worth while, for as he put it, "seeing the gospel in action is the best antidote to any theological aridity." Subsequently, similar missions were arranged during alternate years, and among other places visited have been Gorleston and Romford 1951; Iver, Aylesbury and Stretham Vale, 1953; Bromley, Kilburn, and Plymouth, 1955. In each case, students testified to the value of such missions as part of their own preparation for parochial work, and incumbents wrote of blessing received and Church life strengthened.

A newcomer to the staff in 1949 was the Rev. R. A. Ward, B.D., who had just obtained his London Ph.D. for a thesis on "Aristotelian Usages in the Philosophical Vocabulary of the New Testament." He combined his teaching duties with those of curate at Christ Church, Tunbridge Wells. Another appointment was made as a consequence of the Principal's dissatisfaction with the work being done in speech training. On his recommendation, the Council approved the engagement of the Rev. G. E. Sage, Succentor of St. Paul's Cathedral, as lecturer in this subject. At the same time, a former student and tutor of the College, the Rev. Martin Parsons, Vicar of St. John's, Blackheath, was appointed to the Council. He became Whitehead Professor in 1952, and acquired still closer links with St. John's when the College moved to its new site, through his appointment as Vicar of Emmanuel, Northwood, in 1956; he also became Secretary to the Council on the resignation of Canon T. G. Mohan.

It was not surprising that feelings of frustration should arise through the repeated rejection by successive Ministers of Works of applications for a licence to build the new college. By February, 1949, the architect indicated that such a building as he had designed could hardly now be erected, since building costs were continually rising. Two years later it became clear that modifications of the original plans would be necessary. It was pointed out, however, that this might not be disadvantageous, since changes in the trend of thought within the Church made it wiser to think in terms of accommodating between fifty and sixty men rather than seventy-two.

The death of Bishop Inskip in 1949 brought further acknowledgement by the Council of his "untiring devotion to the College, his successful efforts in obtaining the recognition by the Church of the A.L.C.D., and his unfailing courtesy and kindness," during his twenty-eight years' service, for all but seven of which he had been President and Chairman. Within the year, two further losses were incurred by the deaths of the Rev. H. Earnshaw Smith and of Mr. Albert Mitchell. Appropriate references were made to their services to the College and to the Church as a whole.

Another inspection of the College by representatives of C.A.C.T.M. took place during the Michaelmas Term of 1949. Their report was satisfactory, and the Principal and Staff were congratulated on the standard of work achieved and the devotional spirit prevailing in the College despite the difficulties ensuing from temporary accommodation, which must perforce continue until the new premises were available. By June, 1950, as a result of further representations from London University, the Council approved the appointment of the Principal, in his official capacity, as a member of the Governing Body. Six months later, however, correspondence revealed the dissatisfaction of the University authorities at the distance of the proposed new site at Northwood from London University, and the Academic Registrar urged closer links between College and University. He stated that there was concern at the continued isolation of the College, at the small number of men taking the London B.D., and at the limited help being given by the St. John's staff to the University. In reply to these criticisms, the Principal pointed out that if an additional member of the staff were recognised as a teacher of the University, he would have to be paid a far higher salary than was usual in theological colleges of the Church of England. The number of men taking B.D., however, was likely to increase. The President undertook to inform the Registar that the College also desired closer links with the University, and would endeavour to see in what way these might be attained. In his reply, the Registrar announced recognition of the College for a further five years.

In the summer of 1951 the Vice-Principal, the Rev. R. S. Dean, accepted an invitation to become Principal of Emmanuel College, Saskatoon, in succession to a former Vice-Principal, S. C. Steer, who had recently been consecrated Bishop of Saskatoon. As Dr. Coggan stated in the *Johnian*, Ralph Dean had—

> "thrown himself whole-heartedly into the life of the College, sharing fully in the devotional, evangelical, academic, and recreational parts of our common life. In the period of post-war reconstruction, when St. John's has had to face many grave problems due to the destruction of its old home, our friend's steady counsel and always good-humoured co-operation have meant a very great deal to the well-being of the College, and, I would add, to me personally. . . . We who owe so much to him here will seek to repay a little of our debt by praying for him and his wife [as they go to] a glorious and exacting task."[1]

After five years as Principal, Mr. Dean was consecrated Bishop of Cariboo. He was succeeded as Vice-Principal of St. John's by the Rev. F. H. W. Crabb, a first class London B.D. and former student, who had for nine years been a C.M.S. missionary in the Sudan, and for five of these Principal of Bishop Gwynne College. This he founded and built, starting from the virgin bush, leaving behind a well-established

[1] *Johnian*, Summer Term, 1951.

institution. A new appointment to the Council in June, 1951, was that of Mr. E. F. Starling, A.R.I.B.A., whose expert advice was of great value on many questions connected with the new buildings.

An event which gave great satisfaction occurred in the autumn of 1951, when the Council presented to Mr. Samuel Fuzzard a gift to mark his twenty-five years' association with the College. First appointed by Dr. Gilbert shortly after he arrived as Principal, Fuzzard's tall and purposeful figure soon became a familiar feature of College life. Whether wielding his raucous rattle at 6·45 a.m., serving in the dining-hall, doing innumerable odd jobs, or opening the gate to some late-comer long after dark on winter nights, he served the College well, and not least when, during the war years, he acted as caretaker for the old Highbury buildings.

In February, 1952, the whole country was profoundly shocked at the death of King George VI at Sandringham. It may not be generally remembered that the last clergyman to have the privilege of preaching before him on February 3rd was Canon W. R. Musselwhite, Rector of Wolferton, who was received by His Majesty after the service and invested with the insignia of a Commander of the Royal Victorian Order. Canon Musselwhite was Senior Student of St. John's in 1910, and, writing to another old Johnian, the late Canon A. W. Parsons, he said. "It is a strange and humbling reflection that I should have been allowed to be the last to lay upon his mind some words of strength and comfort from Holy Writ." The College may well be proud and thankful that at such a time one of her sons was in such a privileged position.

During 1952 the Rev. Douglas Webster left the College to become Education Secretary of C.M.S., the Rev. Dr. R. A. Ward to become Professor of New Testament at Wycliffe College, Toronto, and the Rev. R. G. G. Hooper resigned on becoming Vicar of Midhurst. Part-time assistance was received from the Rev. D. W. C. Ford and D. A. Brown, but two further full-time tutors were required. With forty-eight men in residence and the college quite full, such a staff was necessary to deal with the academic work required. In consequence, the Rev. D. C. St. V. Welander, B.D., London, an Old Johnian, and the Rev. J. O'Byrne, B.D., of Trinity College, Dublin, were appointed tutors, and Dr. Coggan was appointed MacNeile professor. It was decided that fees should be raised to £180 per annum.

The year 1953 opened with a decision to ask the architects to modify once again their plans for the new College. They were now instructed to provide for a College of fifty students instead of seventy-five, with bed-sitting-rooms instead of double rooms, in a building of two stories instead of three, the whole to cost £150,000 instead of the original estimate of £212,000. A deputation had again visited Mr. David Eccles, Minister of Works, who expressed his sympathy with the project, but pointed out his difficulty in the light of the urgent claims for many deserving applicants. So the exasperating situation continued, while the College well-wishers watched with dismay the mounting building costs make havoc of their original intentions, without being able to lift a finger to improve matters. In June the Principal rightly stressed to the Council the urgency of getting the new buildings up as quickly as possible:

> "The difficulties of the present set-up are hard to realise unless one is in a position of immediate responsibility in the College. If I mention distance from London, housing facilities for staff and secretarial assistance, it is only to instance three of many problems which constitute a severe strain, and, but for the goodness of God, would jeopardize the life of the College. A minor problem is that the hut at Northwood, where some College goods are stored, is repeatedly being broken into by vandals."

Altogether, it was surprising that efficient College administration and training could be carried on in such strained conditions.

Impressions of life from "below" at this period while confirming such views, reveal that there was a surprisingly keen and united spirit. "Discipline seemed unduly severe and living conditions tough," writes one observer. Life was particularly hard for the considerable contingent of married and older men who came straight out of the Forces after demobilisation, for whom it was in any case difficult to settle down to prolonged study. Radios were not encouraged; the central heating was never switched on, and no coal was distributed until well into November—thus carrying on an old and unloved Highbury tradition! Yet the general level of behaviour was very high, and the spiritual tone good, with a strong sense of fellowship, deep missionary interest and definite evangelistic zeal among most students. The Bible was constantly being expounded both in the chapel and in the lecture-rooms. The Principal did this himself with outstanding skill. No one could pass through St. John's without realising the crucial importance of the Scriptures for the pastoral and preaching ministry. "Chapel services were always reverent, and sometimes inspiring," writes one who was present at this period; "there was no sloppiness or slovenliness. The musical standard was high. It was a great relief when the college hymn-book was changed from the *Church Hymnal* to the revised *Ancient and Modern.*"

Despite the difficulties (and they were many), it became increasingly recognised that a new tradition was being created without wholly discarding the old, by interpreting Evangelical Anglicanism intelligently and relevantly in the world of the mid-twentieth century, and by building up the reputation of the College in the life of the Church of England.

In the autumn of 1953, the College was again full with forty-nine students, of whom two men slept in the village. They represented a good cross-section of English life, with men from such public schools as Eton, Marlborough, Merchant Taylors', Oundle and Christ's Hospital, together with a large number from grammar schools, and several from technical schools. Most had done National Service; one man had retired as a lieutenant-colonel, and another was from the Navy. A clergyman from the Southern Sudan was doing a one-year course, and a German taking the full B.D. course. Nineteen were reading for the B.D., and twenty-five for the A.L.C.D. In Dr. Coggan's opinion, this mixture of background was all to the good, "as the man from the 'orthodox' public school and university background can learn much from the man who comes from workshop or business, and *vice versa*." He also reported a curious situation regarding scholarships; the only applicant for the Peache Scholarship had withdrawn just before the examination because he had grants far in excess of his needs! On the other hand, for some men during their time in College, the financial position worsened, and arrangements were made to give grants from the Harrison-Rogers Memorial Scholarships Fund in certain cases, so bringing that Fund to an end. The Rev. O. R. Brandon, an Old Johnian and M.A. of Bristol University, who had been Rector of Hawkwell, joined the staff this term. He has since been engaged in some important research on the psychology of conversion, his published work being entitled *The Battle for the Soul: Aspects of Religious Conversion.*

There were some who feared that the rural situation at Ford Manor would make it difficult for men to gain experience in practical Christian work. This was far from the case. The Lingfield Epileptic Colony absorbed a large proportion of the students for services in its various homes, but others found a ready welcome at a school for juvenile delinquent boys and at an L.C.C. home for maladjusted boys, where some men shared in the games and club evenings, besides holding short services. Sunday School classes were taken at Hammerwood and at a new housing area, the Stone Quarry Estate, just outside East Grinstead. For hospital work, access was gained to the Queen Victoria Hospital, the plastic surgery centre. The mission experience was therefore of a widely varied character, and fully capable of giving that practical training in pastoral work for which St. John's has always endeavoured to make provision. To quote Mr. Dean once again: "It will be seen that in this rural corner of England, theological students would certainly not live in any ivory tower of unrelated or merely theoretical study."

In April, 1954, the eagerly awaited day arrived; at long last the permit to build was granted. The Council held a meeting of unusual importance on April 26th. Was it coincidence that the first lesson at Morning Prayer had included the passage from Deut. i: "Ye have dwelt long enough in this mount, turn you, and take your journey"? For some of those listening, the words had special significance. After prayer and discussion, it was decided to go forward with the North-wood project without delay, to start work on the site as early as possible in 1955, with a view to completion in 1956. The architect was requested to modify his design so as to give an estimated cost of £175,000. The estimated time for the completion of the building would leave only one year for the lease of Ford Manor, but the Principal felt that, notwithstanding this fact, the College ought to try to be in occupation of the new building by October, 1956, or, if this were not possible, it would then be better to wait till October, 1957. The College Council unanimously decided to "go forward in faith on the basis of a total cost of £210,000, confident that the additional funds would be forthcoming." It was at the same time agreed that a new appeal should be launched for £30,000. The Building Committee was meanwhile engaged in thrashing out such knotty problems as the distractions caused by children of married tutors living over, and playing outside, lecture-rooms and library, and the highly technical decision provoked by the calculation that to reduce the size of each room by six inches would save £2,000! It was decided that no open fires should be installed, the rooms being heated by built-in electric fires. But all these practical details, however important, were never allowed to overshadow the spiritual aspects of the College's life and work. As the Principal wrote:[1]

"A College, however, is not bricks and mortar. Far from it. It is a group of *men* with a common aim and passion. Our motto expresses that aim and

[1] *Johnian*, Summer Term, 1954.

passion—'*Vae mihi si non evangelizavero.*' Circumstances may have ousted us from our old *home.* They have not broken the *College.* . . . New buildings—yes, please God, in the near future. But the same College which for the best part of a century has served God and His Church will, in His goodness, continue that service. Geographical location may change; but the mission of the College remains constant. . . . It is a big venture. Let us meet it boldly and with high courage and foresight. We build for those who come after us. Let us build wisely and nobly. . . . 'The best of all is, God is with us'—that is what I read once again this year on the memorial to the Wesleys in Westminster Abbey. Given that conviction and an infectious enthusiasm, it should not be too big a task to see St. John's, Northwood, rise from firm foundations, and begin a new chapter of its history financially unembarrassed."

In June of this year, the Principal reported on his ten years at the College. During this time one hundred and thirteen men had been ordained, and St. John's was respected by C.A.C.T.M. "as a definitely Evangelical College, which is at the same time loyal to its status as a College of the Anglican Communion." On relations with London University, Dr. Coggan admitted that the authorities had "looked with understanding disapproval at our distance from her." The A.L.C.D. was regarded by the Church as virtually the same as a "pass" degree, while its standard was satisfactory to C.A.C.T.M., but he added:

"If this trend continues, it may mean that the College produces less University of London graduates, and this is likely to displease the authorities. The whole situation is one which needs careful watching and constant reviewing."

Two years later, in June, 1956, the University Senate recommended the recognition of the London College of Divinity as a School of the University in the faculty of theology for a further year, but such recognition was finally withdrawn in 1957.

In connection with the launching of the new appeal in September, 1954, Mr. A. F. Dence was appointed appeal organiser for a period of two years, and a number of Old Johnians were invited to act as regional secretaries. Consideration was given to making a film for publicity purposes, but when it was discovered that this might cost up to £5,000, the scheme was dropped.

At a further inspection by C.A.C.T.M. in 1954, the inspectors expressed their warm approval of work being carried out under difficult conditions, and closed their report with this tribute: "The final impression gained was that Ordinands have here a 'reasonable, holy and lively' training for their Vocation such as we have nowhere seen surpassed and by no means everywhere equalled."

The decision to launch the new appeal for £40,000 (an additional £10,000 was added) was implemented in 1955. Its inauguration took the form of a letter to the *Times* of 6th June, 1955, in the following terms:

"Sir,—The only theological college of the Church of England to suffer irreparable damage in the war was the London College of Divinity, more familiarly known as St. John's Hall, Highbury. Since 1940 its work of training men for the ministry has been carried on in temporary quarters; but at last the opportunity has come to build a new home at Northwood in Middlesex, where the college can again fulfil the obligations and enjoy the privileges of a school of the University of London.

"Four-fifths of the large amount required is already subscribed and in hand; but £40,000 more is needed to complete and equip the buildings, which it is hoped will be ready for occupation early in 1957. The normal resources of the Church of England are fully pledged to bear the heavy burden of providing financial assistance to its candidates who are in training for the ministry. Consequently we must go outside those resources to raise the capital which is still required for the buildings. We therefore request your help in making known our need to a wider public.

Yours faithfully,

✝ Wm. Londin: *Visitor, London College of Divinity*;
Ralph Taylor, Bp., *President*;
Llewellyn Gwynne, Bp., *Honorary Vice-President*;
E. A. Dunn, Prebendary of St. Paul's, *Honorary Vice-President*;
T. G. Mohan, *Honorary Secretary of Council*;
F. Donald Coggan, *Principal*;
A. Frank Dence, *Appeal Organiser*.

London College of Divinity,
Ford Manor,
Lingfield,
Surrey.

A contribution towards the chapel, which was greatly appreciated, was the gift of an east window by Canon Mervyn Glass (1892). This he presented in memory of Dr. Waller. Its design was committed to Mr. Hugh Easton, who had executed the windows in the Memorial Chapel to the Royal Air Force in Westminster Abbey. At the Council meeting in June, 1955, it was agreed that the tender of Messrs. G. E. Wallis and Sons, Ltd., for £181,577 be accepted for the new building, and it was hoped that the appeal would provide for the additional sum needed to complete the project.

The Principal obtained leave of absence from the College during the summer of 1955 to tour East Africa at the invitation of the C.M.S. He visited the four dioceses of Mombasa, the Upper Nile, Sudan and Uganda, travelling some 10,000 miles in three months, conducting clergy retreat conferences and visiting theological colleges and schools. His visit coincided with the campaign against the Mau Mau terrorists, and with a mutiny in the southern Sudan, and so was not without excitement. On his return he emphasised the need in East Africa for more teaching of the faith, and concluded with these significant words: "At a terrifying speed, Africa is being Westernised and modernised. It is an open question whether the Christian Church is keeping pace, *but it will not be an open question for long.*" In the light of subsequent developments, this judgment was indeed prophetic.

During the autumn, the death occurred of Prebendary Hinde, who had been a Council member for thirty-three years, Secretary for nineteen, and Vice-Chairman since 1945. He had also been acting Principal from 1942 to 1944. His great services to the Church and to the College were recalled with gratitude. He was succeeded on the Council by Professor J. N. D. Anderson, O.B.E., LL.D., of London University, and as Vice-Chairman by Canon St. John Thorpe.

It was on Saturday, October 15th, 1955, that the foundation stone of the new St. John's Hall, Northwood, was laid by one of the most distinguished of all Old Johnians, the Rt. Rev. Llewellyn H. Gwynne, C.M.G., D.D., formerly Bishop in Egypt. The marquee was more than filled by the large number of guests, which included members of the College Council, representatives of the local civic authorities, and many other invited friends of the College. The President (the Right Rev. J. R. S. Taylor) referred in his address to the College's years of wandering since the war, but now its new and permanent home was rising, and it was appropriate that one of the most honoured members of the College, who was also "one of the outstanding missionary bishops of our generation" should lay the first stone. Thereupon the ninety-two-year-old bishop, having placed the stone in position, said in clear tones: "To the glory of God, and in the faith of Jesus Christ, I lay this stone." The hymns "Praise to the Holiest in the Height" and "Christ is our Corner-stone" were led by a choir formed from student members of the College, who also sang Ps. cxxvii. The Bishop of

Barking (the Right Rev. Hugh Gough, O.B.E.) read the prayers, and the Principal read the lesson.

A few days later, on October 26th, *The Times* carried the announcement of the resignation of Dr. Coggan as Principal on his appointment to the Bishopric of Bradford. It will not be out of place to quote from the appreciation of Dr. Coggan written in the *Johnian* by the College President, Bishop J. R. S. Taylor:

"Four qualities have impressed me most. First, the cheerful courage with which he has faced the many difficulties and limiting circumstances of this 'exile' period. Secondly, his never-failing consideration for the comfort and welfare of other people, for his teaching staff, for his domestic helpers and for the students individually. Then, his co-operation in the life and fellowship of the Hall. And I have noticed the same spirit in his wider contacts in the Church. And, lastly, his conscientiousness, that quality without which none can become great. This I have observed in his faithfulness to duty and in the thoroughness he gives to the details of his administration and teaching work alike. . . . We rejoice that his rich gifts will find a wider sphere and meet a greater need in the Diocese of Bradford, where we shall follow him with our prayers."

Dr. Coggan's work had indeed been a triumph over adverse conditions throughout his time as Principal. War and its aftermath, with the continual struggle to cope with the material difficulties of food and fuel rationing in improvised quarters, domestic staff problems, the distance from London and maintaining good relations with C.A.C.T.M. and London University—these added to the academic and spiritual leadership which must devolve upon every theological college principal, made a burden which might well have daunted any man. But the way in which Dr. Coggan was able to surmount these and other problems, leaving to his successor a compact and flourishing College, about to embark on new expansion in greatly improved surroundings, indicate those qualities recognised by his election first to the See of Bradford and then to that of York. Some, of course, had reservations. It was said that he did not take his staff sufficiently into his confidence about matters discussed at Council meetings; nor were the opinions of his colleagues sought about staff appointments or the curacies to which men might suitably go. Others felt that the students could have been given more information on matters affecting College life. No doubt, if true, he had good reasons for reticence, and certainly he would have been following traditional College policy in this respect. But, this being said, it is clear that during the Lingfield period the College became widely known, and increasingly received the confidence of the bishops. This was undoubtedly due above all else to Dr. Coggan's personality and enthusiasm. Nor should Mrs. Coggan's contribution be overlooked. A year alone in Canada in 1944-5, followed by further periods of separation from her husband for family reasons during the Lingfield years, were all cheerfully accepted, while staff and students will remember with gratitude her hospitality and interest.

It was curiously prophetic that in the lesson at the foundation-stone laying ceremony Dr. Coggan should read: "I have laid the foundation, and another buildeth thereon." In his eleven and a half years as Principal, he had indeed laid the foundation of the new St. John's; it would now be left to another to complete the building, and to continue the work which he had developed with such conspicuous success. Dr. Coggan continued as Principal until January, 1956. The Vice-Principal, the Rev. F. H. W. Crabb, was then appointed acting Principal, and held this office until the end of the academic year.

In February, 1956, the Council appointed the Rev. Hugh Jordan as Principal. A specialist in Hebrew, Mr. Jordan was a B.D. of Trinity College, Dublin, and brought to his new post the fruits of wide experience both in Ireland and England. Ordained to a curacy in Dublin, he then became for five years General Secretary of the city of Dublin Y.M.C.A. Ten years of parochial work followed in Lancashire and Staffordshire, after which, in 1949, he was appointed Vicar of Redland, Bristol, and lecturer at Tyndale Hall, so was no stranger to academic work. For one year he presided over the College at Ford Manor, and was then responsible for the move to Northwood, with the considerable administrative problems involved in the changeover. Other changes at this time included the resignation of the Council Secretary, the Rev. T. G. (now Canon) Mohan, and the appointment of the Rev. L. E. H. Stephens-Hodge as chaplain and tutor. Mr. Stephens-Hodge had gained a first class in the Theological Tripos at Cambridge, and had had experience of parochial work, both in England and Scotland. In June, 1957, Mr. Crabb resigned as Vice-Principal on being appointed Principal of Emmanuel College, Saskatoon, thus forging yet a further link between this college and St. John's. The Council conveyed to him their profound thanks for his work during the preceding five years, and offered their sincere good wishes for his new work in Canada. He was succeeded as Vice-Principal by the Rev. A. V. McCallin, who, like the new Principal, came from Ireland. A scholar in philosophy, senior Moderator in Mental and Moral Science, and

B.D. of Trinity College, Dublin, his previous ministry had been spent entirely in Northern Ireland.

Work on the new buildings made satisfactory progress, and by the summer of 1957 it was clear that the date arranged for the opening of the College early in October would not need to be postponed. The Michaelmas term began with the various inauguration ceremonies. The official opening was on Thursday, October 10th. When all had been arranged and rehearsed to the last detail, everyone was shocked to learn that the previous evening Bishop Montgomery Campbell of London had suffered slight concussion in a motor accident, and would be unable to dedicate the new chapel. After hasty telephone calls, the Archbishop of Canterbury (Dr. Fisher) kindly consented not only to declare the College open, but also to dedicate the chapel, and the Bishop of Bradford agreed to preach the sermon. Once more a vast concourse of people gathered at Northwood: the Vice-Chancellor of London University, principals of other theological colleges, representatives of the Press and of local organisations, members of the College Council, architects, builders, and Old Johnians in profusion, of whom none was more welcome than Bishop Gwynne, who at ninety-four years of age was probably the oldest living Johnian, being born in the year the College was founded—1863!

The ceremony took place in the dining-hall with the President, Bishop J. R. S. Taylor in the chair. In expressing thanks to all who had helped forward the building project, he mentioned especially three gifts in the chapel; the east window, given by Canon Mervyn Glass in memory of Dr. Waller, the dorsal curtains given by the Bishop of Bradford, and silver alms dish presented by the architects of the new College, Messrs. Fielding Dodd and Stevens. The Archbishop's speech, in his usual humorous and genial vein, did much to make a rather complicated programme run smoothly and happily. At the dedication service in chapel, robed clergy included the new Bishop of Stepney, the Right Rev. Evered Lunt, an Old Johnian, besides the President, the Archbishop of Canterbury, the Bishop of Bradford and the College staff. Dr. Coggan took for his text Ps. xliv. 3.

"We look back," he said, "over days marked by considerable anxieties, but marked also by constant signs of God's goodness. We realise that we have not got this place in possession by our own strength, but God's right hand, His arm and the light of His countenance have brought it about. We have learnt something of the meaning of glory through suffering, that great theme of the Fourth Gospel which Hugh Easton has so wonderfully immortalised in the window which is the main feature of the east end of this chapel. We ascribe to God, as are most justly due, all thanks, might, majesty and glory."

Two days later, the Principal, staff and students were at home to their friends and neighbours, and many expressions of appreciation were heard of the dignity and simplicity of the new College. October 15th was the Old Johnians' day, when some 120 members of the Clerical Union gathered at the new building for their reunion. At the service of Holy Communion, Bishop Taylor preached on the text: "They dwelt with the King for his work" (I Chron. iv. 23), speaking of the King's reign, of his work, in which we are all called to share, and of His guests, who are made welcome at His Table. At the meeting afterwards, with E. T. Hughes in the chair, a few selected Johnians of various decades briefly recalled their memories of College life. The closing speaker, the Rev. Martin Parsons, chose rather to look forward, and set the tone for the work of the College lying ahead. As Evangelicals, he said, we were out, not to form a party, but to win men for Jesus Christ. To the staff he said: "Produce men who have learnt to worship the Lord in the beauty of holiness, men of prayer, men who will go wherever God will send them"; and to all Old Johnians: "Recapture your hopes and visions of long ago, and let this new beginning here in Northwood be for you a new beginning in your own work and ministry." So the opening ceremonies ended on a note of high endeavour, which has been amply fulfilled.

In the succeeding years, under Mr. Jordan's able leadership, the College has gone forward and prospered. At the moment of writing, it is "bursting at the seams" with seventy-three students, and once again the problem is that of accommodation. In 1960, the Rev. E. M. B. Green joined the staff. Abbot Scholar and Exhibitioner of Exeter College, Oxford, Mr. Green took a first in "Greats," and then migrated to Cambridge, where he took a first class in the Theological Tripos Part III (New Testament), and gained the Carus Greek Testament Prize—a brilliant academic record. He came to Northwood from a curacy at Holy Trinity, Eastbourne.

In the spring of 1961, Bishop Taylor resigned as Chairman of the College Council, after holding that office through fifteen eventful years. He was succeeded as Chairman by the Right Rev. Russell White, Suffragan Bishop of Tonbridge, who, as Secretary of the Evangelical Churchmen's Ordination Council for over twenty-five years and as a member of the Council of C.A.C.T.M., had been closely associated with ordination training. The death of Bishop Taylor in December,

1961, called forth many tributes to the value of his work as an Evangelical leader. The Archbishop of York, preaching at his memorial service in All Souls' Church, Langham Place, on January 24th, 1962, stated:

"The greatest influence of his life was on boys and young men. This is not to underestimate the importance of his four years as Rector of a country town, nor his eleven years as a diocesan bishop. It is only to emphasise the greatness of the influence which he exercised on a vast number of young men at the most critical and formative periods of their lives. . . . There was in him an element of the rock-like, the tenacity to truth as he saw it and loved it. But always with this there went a courtesy and graciousness which, to me at least, was the most outstanding of his qualities. . . . He had great funds of strength available for others' problems, as I proved again and again in facing with him the perplexities of reconstruction after the years of war havoc. His serenity had its roots deep in his faith in God as his Father, in Christ as Saviour, and in the Holy Spirit as Sanctifier. It was nourished in an intensely happy life-partnership and in family affection. This it was which brought him deep content when the pressures upon him were constant and demanding."

It was fortunate indeed that St. John's had the benefit of his wise and shrewd guidance in years which were among the most difficult in its history. Under his presidency the large sum of £210,000 for the college rebuilding was completed. This consisted of the proceeds of the sale of the old College to the Arsenal Football Club, together with the other savings put aside year by year as a reserve fund, to which was added compensation for fire damage. Towards the remaining £40,000, £20,000 was raised by direct gifts in response to the Appeal, and the remainder came by way of grants from the Church Commissioners, from trusts, and from the sale of some surplus land at Northwood.

As it reaches its centenary, the College may well look back with gratitude on the way of God's leading. Through paths sometimes rough, and over many unexpected obstacles, the work has continued from the days of its humble origins. As in other and wider spheres, it exemplifies God's basic principle of dealing with men by continuity through change. Kilburn, Highbury, Wadhurst, Oak Hill, Harrow, Lingfield, Northwood—each name now falls into place in the College chronicle. But though varied in their setting, and in the many memories which they evoke, they have one thing in common; that always and in every place, men learned and grew in the knowledge and in the love of God as they prepared for the ministry to which they believed that He had called them.

"We have this treasure in earthen vessels, that the excellency of the power may be of God and not of us."[1]

St. Paul's words still ring true; whether the treasure is enshrined in the earthen vessels of different buildings or geographical localities, or in human hearts differing widely in talent, temperament and personality, yet it remains the same throughout all ages. In a remote west Norfolk churchyard is a tombstone in memory of a clergyman who gave many years of service to the Church in England and in India. It bears this inscription:

"The end for which he lived was to make men see the light of the knowledge of the glory of God in the face of Jesus Christ."

To that end the College still labours, conscious that it will only achieve its high purpose as and when each man going forth from its walls can say with reverent lips, out of a full heart, and from a depth of personal experience:

"Necessity is laid upon me; yea, woe is me if I preach not the gospel!"

[1] II Cor. iv. 7.

PART II

Men in the Ministry

CHAPTER VI

"For the Work of the Ministry"

I F it is true to say that the reputation and prestige of a theological college depends largely on its principal, it is equally true that, in a wider sense, such reputation depends upon the life and work of each man who goes forth from it. To a remarkable extent the ordinary churchgoer will judge a college by the character and conduct of its former students. St. John's may not boast of many "great" names from the human standpoint. Though some are set in the Church to be apostles and prophets, others are set to be pastors, teachers, evangelists —and "helps." The majority are no doubt included in this last category, yet a number of former students have been called upon to assume high responsibility in the Church's life and ministry. In grateful recollection of what such men have done, or are doing, and for the encouragement which their faithful witness must bring, the following examples are given for the purposes of this record of the College's contribution to the work of the Ministry.

It is just over 100 years since John Edwin Watts-Ditchfield was born on September 17th, 1861. His parents were Methodists, his father being a schoolmaster in Patricroft, Lancashire. When he was thirteen years old he experienced conversion, and at the age of sixteen preached his first sermon on the text Acts ix. 6: "And he trembling and astonished said, Lord, what wilt Thou have me to do?" These words might well have been his own when a few years later he was rejected as a candidate for the Methodist ministry. This decision came as a complete surprise and bitter disappointment, for he had finished his training at Headingly, Leeds, successfully passing his examinations, when he was told in effect that he was regarded as redundant, there being more students than vacancies for ministers—a curious situation to modern Anglican ears! Advised to offer for work in South Africa, he found that door similarly closed. A few months after this, in November, 1888, Watts-Ditchfield turned to the Church of England, and was confirmed in

Manchester Cathedral by Bishop Moorhouse. His previous experience of Methodism, however, left him with a broad-minded outlook and sympathy with those of differing views, though throughout his life he maintained his definite Evangelical convictions.

His earlier call to the Ministry now returned to his mind, but financial considerations made a university degree out of the question. He therefore adopted the unusual course of acting as Secretary to the Rev. J. Pullein Thompson, Vicar of St. Stephen's, North Bow, while attending lectures at St. John's, Highbury, as an external student under Dr. Waller. In 1891 he was ordained by Bishop Frederick Temple of London to the curacy of St. Peter's, Upper Holloway, under the Rev. J. F. Osborne, where he remained for five years. Here he quickly gave evidence of unusual gifts in working among men. He began a carefully advertised weekly men's service, with such arresting titles as "Rifle Shots," "Long Odds," "The Crooked Woman," "Notice to Quit," and he preached to crowded congregations, many of whom had come to church for the first time in their lives. Numerous conversions followed among those who had formerly been notorious drunkards and even criminals. Watts-Ditchfield did much for the welfare of the people by inaugurating a Sick, Burial and Annual Distribution Society, together with a Christmas Club, while the intellectual needs of his flock were catered for by the setting up of a reading-room and library. As a counter-attraction to the public houses, he opened a club with games-room, where chess and bagatelle could be played, and he organised athletic activities and competitions for those who cared to take part.

But his chief work was in the field of parochial visiting, where his persistence and hard work brought great rewards. On one occasion he saw a man trying to escape through the back door as he went in at the front. He ran through the house, and confronted the startled man with the words: "Do you know that this is your centenary?" The man asked what he meant, and was told: "This is the one hundredth visit I have paid you." The man was so ashamed that he accepted the invitation to come to church the following Sunday, and experienced conversion. So hard did Watts-Ditchfield labour that his friends feared that he would have a breakdown. They therefore persuaded him to tour Egypt and Palestine during the autumn and winter of 1896-7. During this time of travel through the places identified with our Lord's life and work, he spent much time in meditation and prayer, in the course of which the conviction grew that he was destined for another and wider sphere of service. It was therefore hardly a surprise when, shortly after his return, he was offered in February, 1897, by the Bishop of London (Mandell Creighton) the slum parish of St. James the Less, Bethnal Green. Here some 11,000 people were living in the most sordid conditions, many of the men being casual labourers in the docks, while their wives and daughters worked in neighbouring factories. The work represented a tremendous challenge, and Watts-Ditchfield threw himself whole-heartedly into his new task. His first objective was the church, then in a poor state of repair, and he succeeded in raising £4,000 mainly from outside sources, for its restoration. It was almost completely destroyed by enemy action during the Second World War.

Next he concentrated upon the men, starting men's services which once again attracted large congregations, drawing in as before many who had previously had no contact with any church. He also held open-air services in Victoria Park, enlarged the Sunday schools, and organised the parish into districts, each with its own visitor. Life was hard, and work was tough in the early days of this century, and the East End of London was as difficult a sphere in which to live and work as anywhere in the country. But he was determined that his people should not be parochially minded, and by adopting G. W. Wright as "own missionary" (afterwards Bishop of Sierra Leone and of North Africa), he taught that a live Church is a missionary Church. Year by year £200 was subscribed for this purpose, made up almost entirely of coppers.

Despite his heavy parochial commitments, Watts-Ditchfield found time for many additional interests. His work as Secretary to the College Council of St. John's, and in the foundation of St. John's College, Durham, has already been mentioned. Somehow, amid his ceaseless activities, he found time to write, and his work, *Fishers of Men*, first published in 1899, was long regarded as a standard work on how to run men's services. In 1913 Cambridge University selected him for the post of Lecturer in Pastoral Theology, of which opportunity he took full advantage. The lectures were later published under the title, *The Church in Action*. He had for some time been closely identified with the Church of England Men's Society, and in 1912 left as the Society's missioner for a long tour of Australia and New Zealand, visiting the chief centres of population, and returning via the Pacific and across Canada. He was away for eight months, and his mission was an immense success, large numbers everywhere attending the services and meetings. "He carried men away," wrote the Archbishop of Sydney

(J. C. Wright), "by his downright spiritual earnestness and his buoyant enthusiasm." (*The Times*, July 16th, 1923.) His curate, the Rev. (later Prebendary) E. A. Dunn, also an Old Johnian, took charge of the parish most efficiently in his absence.

Within two months of his return, he was astonished to receive on January 27th, 1914, a letter from the Prime Minister inviting him to become the first Bishop of the new Diocese of Chelmsford. "No university career," he wrote, "brought up a Methodist, not even a resident student of Highbury, yet my life has been shaped by God in this week. It is really wonderful. . . . Here am I, O Lord; what wouldst Thou have me to do?"[1] His old College rejoiced, with many hundreds of his friends, at the appointment of their first representative as an English diocesan bishop, and their prayers followed him at his consecration on February 24th, 1914. Years of ceaseless activity followed; at first they were years of war, when he was frequently called upon to minister to the bereaved, and proved himself a real "Father in God." Being convinced of the justice of the Allied cause, he did not shrink from pleading for recruits in the days before conscription was introduced, despite criticism in certain quarters. He also incurred hostility by a series of fearless and outspoken addresses in St. Paul's Cathedral during Holy Week in 1916, in the course of which he called attention to the neglect of Sunday, and the prevalence of intemperance, gambling and bad housing. And he went on: "In the craze for ease, people are demanding short sermons, short services, etc., but what we need is the religion of the Cross and a life of self-denial." In a striking passage he stated:

> "England will never be saved by conscription, by munitions, by wealth. These things may help, if used by a nation full of soul; but England will only be saved by her soul-power. It is soul-power that dominates the world."

When the war was over, he gave his utmost support to the Enabling Act of 1919, by which the Church Assembly was constituted, with powers to prepare and present ecclesiastical legislation to Parliament. He embarked on a great teaching campaign, so that the machinery of the Church in his diocese might become efficient to meet the new demands laid upon it, and to make full use of the opportunities afforded by the measure. He also called for a great effort to raise funds to set the new diocese on its feet, raising many thousands of pounds for the building of new churches and vicarages and for the augment-

[1] E. N. Gowing, *John Edwin Watts-Ditchfield*, p. 132.

ation of stipends. It had been feared that, owing to his pronounced Evangelical convictions, Watts-Ditchfield would discriminate against Anglo-Catholics, but by 1920 even the *Church Times* (October 15th) was found admitting:

> "It would be idle to pretend that the views of the Bishop of Chelmsford are on all points identical with those of Catholics, but he is no partisan in the narrow sense of the term. . . . He possesses to an extraordinary degree the power of appreciating those whose beliefs differ from his own, and of respecting convictions which he does not share."

Among Evangelicals he sought to mediate between "conservative" and "liberals," particularly at the time of the unfortunate schism in 1922 in the C.M.S., to which society he always remained loyal. But in the midst of these arduous duties, the Bishop died suddenly after an operation in July, 1923. Tributes to his work were at once forthcoming from many quarters. The Bishop of Barking (J. T. Inskip) preaching shortly afterwards at Chelmsford Cathedral said: "His largeness of heart, his tolerant spirit, his grasp of great subjects, his desire to draw men together, gave him a wonderful influence which will be missed terribly in solving the problems which beset us." And *The Times* expressed the feelings of many people when it wrote:

> "Though he was a very strong Evangelical, he knew how to adapt his message to the varying capacities and needs of plain men. His sermons were marked by a shrewdness which made them level to the experience of his congregation. He won the respect of the huge artisan population of the diocese and the clergy quickly recognised his desire to help them in parishes which are in many cases as difficult as any in England" (July 16th, 1923).

St. John's may indeed recall with pride her first English diocesan, for he exemplified so many of those ideals for which the College was founded.

Next we turn to one whose contribution to the Church is well known, Prebendary Wilson Carlile. He was born in Brixton in January, 1847, the eldest of twelve children. Not physically robust in childhood, he set himself by sheer determination, attention to exercise and diet, to overcome this disability, and with such success that when well over ninety, he still could do a full day's work. His grandfather, a prosperous silk-merchant, had built up a flourishing business in Cheapside, which Wilson Carlile entered in September, 1862, and spent sixteen years in the commercial world, developing a talent for organisation and detail, and also revealing both industry and ambition as he became virtual manager of the business. His schoolboy dream of making £20,000 before he was twenty-five years of age met with such success that for many years he never put aside less than £2,000 per annum. His work involved travel in many parts of the Continent, but for religion, and the world of ideals bound up in the term, he cared nothing. As a matter of form, he was admitted at eighteen to membership of the Stockwell Congregational Church (in which General and Mrs. Booth of the Salvation Army had been married), but he did not feel that this demanded any profession of personal faith. The experience of seeing many badly wounded men in the Franco-Prussian War of 1870-1 led him to consider the philosophy of Kant in its relation to life and death, but here he found little to satisfy him.

The change came with a financial crisis in 1873, when quite suddenly the young man of twenty-six, with a capital of some £30,000 and owner of a prosperous and expanding business, found himself after the crash to be worth a mere £1,500. There followed a period of physical and nervous prostration, and he had to spend some weeks on his back with spinal trouble, the recurrence of a childhood weakness. "God threw me on my back that I might look up the better," he said later, speaking of this experience. The visits of an aunt, a devout Christian, and his own enforced inactivity, led him to feel that the world offered something more than gold to live for. One day she presented him with a small book, and urged him to read it; it was Mackay's *Grace and Truth*. "At the beginning of the chapter," he said, "I was a rank outsider; before I got to the end, I had thrown myself at the feet af Christ, and cried, 'My Lord and my God.' "[1] For Carlile, a devotion to winning money was now turned to a devotion to winning men. He threw up his business and in due course, after a brief sojourn among the Plymouth Brethren, he and his wife were confirmed by Bishop Thorold of Rochester in Clapham Parish Church, Carlile henceforth devoting his spare time from working in his father's business to holding services for young men in an old schoolroom belonging to the parish of Holy Trinity, Richmond, whose Vicar was the Rev. Evan Hopkins.

His "Rough Sunday School," as it came to be called, stimulated his appetite for this kind of work, but it was through being brought into contact with the Moody and Sankey mission of 1875, and in particular with one who was assisting them, Professor Henry Drummond, that the way was opened for the next momentous stage in his life. Obliged to address a large meeting at short notice, Carlile was suddenly possessed

[1] A. E. Reffold, *Wilson Carlile and the Church Army*, p. 28.

with the idea that laymen could be taught to preach Christ. From that moment he longed to see earnest young men, recognised by the Church, preaching in the market-place and on the village green. It was now that his life-long love of music was put to good use, for he was appointed to train the Camberwell Choir, as it was called, for Moody's South London Campaign. This continued after the mission under the name of the London Evangelistic Choir, with Carlile, its leader, singing solos and preaching, and frequently taking part with his famous trombone.

But he remained unsatisfied with such opportunities of service, and in 1878 was accepted by Dr. Boultbee as a student at St. John's Highbury. In Lent, 1880, he was ordained by Bishop Jackson of London to the curacy of St. Mary Abbot, Kensington, under the Rev. Carr Glyn (later Bishop of Peterborough). Here, among a band of ten curates representing all Church parties, High, Low and Broad, Carlile learned the importance of tolerance and understanding in the interests of one great work. At once he began to hold open-air services in the poorest and most squalid districts, and even in Kensington High Street—a novelty in a fashionable West End parish—at the same time visiting the Guards and police depots. But it was the multitudes who never darkened a church's door which troubled him most; his efforts to reach them were concentrated in his open-air work, in whose conduct he encouraged his lay supporters to take some part, however small. In time his mission church became filled, and his helpers were gradually persuaded to give brief addresses. This led to opposition, and even to scuffles, with organised gangs trying to break up the meetings. At length the Vicar received so many complaints from members of his congregation, and from neighbouring shopkeepers, that he commanded Carlile to discontinue them. But he secured a meeting between his curate and Canon Hay Aitken of the Church Parochial Mission Society. Eventually that Society agreed to accept representatives of all parties on its Committee, Wilson Carlile being appointed Chief Secretary of a sub-committee to direct the Church Army, as his new organisation was now called. By 1883 he had moved to the slums of Westminster, where he and his devoted supporters suffered every sort of indignity and assault, and constant ill-usage, being pelted with flour, red ochre and stones. But still they carried on, and within two years had extended their work be establishing a Training House at Oxford, with the support of Bishop Mackarness. Later this moved to London, setting up headquarters in the Edgware Road. Earlier suspicion and misunder-standing of its work was dispelled when it became clear that definite

Church teaching was given, that evangelists never went into parishes uninvited by the incumbent; neither did they stay if the incumbent wished them to leave.

Gradually the Church Army separated from the Church Parochial Mission Society, becoming a distinct and self-contained Society, receiving increasing recognition and support, until, within a few years, it became established as an important handmaid of the Church. Many incumbents today can testify to the valuable services rendered in their parishes by its Captains and Sisters, while royal patronage was extended to its work. In 1905, Wilson Carlile was appointed a Prebendary of St. Paul's by Bishop Winnington Ingram of London, and in 1915 he was given the unusual distinction of being awarded the honorary degree of Doctor of Divinity by Oxford University. But the most gratifying honour of all was paid to him when King George V made him a Companion of Honour in 1926. At his funeral in St. Paul's Cathedral on October 3rd, 1942, the Archbishop of Canterbury, William Temple, declared that Carlile "saw a vision of a Church brought into living contact with those who, at that time, largely remained untouched by its influence." *The Times* report continued:

> "The inspiration was that of one man whom they honoured that day. It might well be doubted whether any man in their communion in the last two generations had done so much to bring the Gospel home as a living force to the hearts and lives of their fellow countrymen, and to many more beyond the seas."

Wilson Carlile's portrait showing him with his beloved trombone, occupies a prominent place in the College dining-hall.

Another eminent representative of the College, ordained in 1897, whose reminiscences have already been recorded, is Bishop Thomas Sherwood Jones, who served the whole of his ministry in the northern province, gaining a Durham B.A. after he left St. John's Hall. His great work was as Rector of Middleton from 1920 to 1945, where he was also Rural Dean for fifteen years. He was consecrated Suffragan Bishop of Hulme in 1930, while continuing to hold his incumbency, and in 1931 received an honorary D.D. from Durham University. His younger son was consecrated Assistant Bishop of Lagos in 1944, but died in Nigeria in 1948.

A suffragan bishop very much on the active list is Bishop Evered Lunt of Stepney. After ordination in the Oxford Diocese in 1925, he served curacies in Maidenhead and Cambridge before being appointed in 1934 chaplain to the Cambridge Pastorate and Chaplain of Downing College. From 1943 to 1951 he was Rector of St. Aldate's, Oxford, and here he exercised a further most fruitful University ministry, still remembered for its pastoral value by many former undergraduates. When in 1951 he was offered the Deanery of Bristol, he found himself once more involved in the life of a great University, where, as he writes, "the atmosphere was a fascinating mingling of the ancient and modern, and where one exercised a fourfold ministry to the Diocese, the Cathedral, the city and the University." In 1957, he became Bishop of Stepney, with special responsibility for the East End, and he continues:

> "It would be impossible here to do more than make a passing reference to a work at once so difficult and so stimulating, and to pay a tribute, all too inadequate, to the band of clergy and other fellow workers with whom I am privileged to work, from whom I learn so much, and so many of whom have become my personal friends."

And what can one more say of those who have passed on, or who are still in active work? Of men like Canon A. W. Parsons, whose pastoral ministry in Leicester and Boscombe is still gratefully recalled; of Canon S. M. Warner, whose faithful ministry at Holy Trinity, Eastbourne, drew such large congregations; of B. W. Isaac, for many years associated with the Church Pastoral Aid Society; of E. H. Wade, who after a chaplaincy at Downing College, Cambridge, went to South Africa, and became Archdeacon of Durban; he now holds the post of General Secretary to the United Society for Christian Literature; of Ivan Neill, the present Chaplain-General to the Forces, and of Norman Motley and his Othona Community; of Brian Hession, who founded Cancer Anonymous, and fought a great fight before succumbing to that dread disease himself; of Canon Bryan Green, Rector of Birmingham, who by his writings and his evangelistic campaigns is known in many parts of the world as a gifted evangelist, especially used among young people. Some, admittedly, have in the course of years identified themselves with views or with movements for which their College training hardly prepared them: one became Secretary of the English Church Union; another was a leading figure in the strange sect of the Agapemonites at the end of the last century. But perhaps the list may be closed by reference to one who has given long and valued service in the London Diocese, E. A. Dunn. He was ordained in 1902 to the curacy of St. James the Less, Bethnal Green, and his work as assistant to Watts-Ditchfield has already been mentioned. He became incumbent of the parish from 1914 to 1918, in which year he moved to All Souls', Harlesden. His only appointment outside the London Diocese was as perpetual curate of St. Jude's, Nottingham, from 1927 to 1931. In 1931 he returned to London as Vicar of St. James', Muswell Hill, where he remained until his retirement in 1958, being made Prebendary of Caddington Minor in St. Paul's Cathedral in 1939.

A bare list of appointments conveys little idea of the worth of this long ministry, but one of his curates, the present Bishop of St. Edmundsbury and Ipswich, paid this tribute to Prebendary Dunn's life and work in 1962, the diamond jubilee year of his ordination. Dr. Morris writes:

"I joined the staff of Prebendary (then the Reverend) E. A. Dunn when he was Vicar of All Souls', Harlesden, the great railway parish with its centre at Willesden Junction, as a deacon at Trinity, 1922. I was particularly happy to receive the offer of my title from Mr. Dunn; I had known of his wonderful work as a curate of the Rev. J. E. Watts-Ditchfield (later Bishop of Chelmsford) at St. James the Less, Bethnal Green. No young deacon could have had a finer training. His staff consisted at that time of three curates and two lady workers. The Vicar was an indefatigable worker who never spared himself or his staff. His own example of industry, attention to detail and efficiency demanded in return everything one had to give. My memories of my one and only curacy are of being welcomed by the Vicar and Mrs. Dunn as a member of the family and of being treated as such throughout very nearly four years of our work together. A few special points stand out as marking him out as one of the most outstanding parish priests of his time.

"First and foremost, he was a winner of souls, and a wonderful trainer of curates in consequence. I recall how he gave up his time to take me visiting with him during my first month in the parish to show me how pastoral visiting should be done. He never failed to indicate that pastoral visitation was not just a matter of a social call; it was natural to him to take tea with a family and pray with them without any sense of incongruity or even embarrassment.

"His outstanding work was among men, and his great Sunday-afternoon services for men were his special joy. It was quite a usual thing in those days to have 800 or 1,000 men in church every Sunday, and the whole staff of curates was detailed to visit public houses in the parish on Saturday nights. The purpose of these services, and similar women's services on Monday nights, was to bring men and women into a full communicant life of the Church.

"The Vicar trusted the members of his staff to do their work, gave them a free hand to use their own initiative, but never failed, if appealed to, to give help and guidance. He was always anxious to give praise to others, and never failed to support his staff. He was a natural leader, and in great demand as a preacher and speaker. He always showed Christian love and charity to those whose views differed from his own, and yet in matters of principle stood firm on the evangelical basis of his own convictions.

"Looking back over the years and still enjoying the warm personal friendship of my old Vicar in his retirement, I feel that the London College of Divinity has good reason to be very proud of this distinguished former student, who in his day and generation is probably one of the most beloved clergymen in the Church of England. Respected by all schools of thought in the Church, hundreds of men and women owe to him a vision of our Lord which was given to them by Prebendary Dunn, a man of prayer, with a great love of Jesus Christ revealed in all his dealings with those committed to his care."

It may just be added that in 1952 Archbishop Fisher broke his rule of never returning to his former diocese, in order to be present and preach at the crowded service to mark the jubilee of Prebendary Dunn's ordination, where some 1,200 people at St. James' heard a glowing appreciation of one whose work the Archbishop had seen at close quarters during his time as Bishop of London.

If it appears invidious to have made any selection when the work of so many Johnians has contributed to the life of the Church, yet, as many would be the first to acknowledge, Prebendary Dunn well represents a great company of men who for 100 years have borne witness to those principles for which the College was founded. Mining areas and industrial districts, seaside resorts and country villages, market towns and cathedral cities—to all alike have men gone forth from the London College of Divinity bearing the same message of a gospel to meet the needs of all men, confronting them with that good news which is now and always "the very power of God working for the salvation of everyone who believes it."[1]

[1] Rom. i. 16 (J. B. Phillips).

CHAPTER VII

"Into All the World"

WHAT mysterious power lies behind that word "Vigiles" to a multitude of old Johnians! The original idea was in fact attributed to D. A. Canney. In the summer of 1888 he met with a few others in the study of S. A. Johnston to pray for the work of the Church overseas, though already there were missionary prayer groups in the College. In fact, Bishop Gwynne claimed to have been to such a group with the future Bishop Taylor Smith as early as 1883. From the beginning Dr. Gee of the tutorial staff showed deep interest in the young society, and indeed was responsible for choosing its title. Its objective, and rules for its conduct were duly formulated and drawn up, and the inaugural meeting of the Vigiles Union was held on February 14th, 1890, so emphasising still further the application of the College motto in a world-wide context.

The Union quickly gained wide support, and within a few years its Secretaryship became a recognised College office. One of its aims was to link together missionary-minded Johnians in home parishes by asking them if they would be prepared to give occasional sermons and addresses on behalf of the missionary cause—indeed, to undertake the kind of work now done by organising secretaries and missionaries on furlough. This lesser-known side of the Vigiles activities seems to have continued for some eleven years or more. But the society's main aims have always been to stimulate missionary interest within the College, and to keep in touch with Johnians on the mission field. One of the original rules was to pray once a week for those members of the College engaged in foreign missionary work; another was to read missionary literature for at least half an hour each week (or else, in default, to place one penny in the missionary box!). In these two rules appear the basic principles of Vigiles intercession—namely, informed prayer. At first the meeting was held one evening per week, but it was soon transferred, in the spirit of true "Watchmen," to an early hour of the morning in the "Cab Rank" of the chapel. One has left on record that he never knew which was the worse sin—to miss Vigiles or to suffer from spiritual pride if he attended! For over seventy years the faithful have gathered at these meetings, nowadays held at 6.35 a.m. A short talk is given sketching the needs of a particular area, usually by students, but sometimes by visiting missionaries, followed by prayer, and attendance is often near the twenty mark. A Vigiles library has been in existence for some years, to stimulate interest and study by providing specialised information.

But the underlying strength of the society lies not so much in information as in the personal links with Johnians throughout the world, and part of the stimulus to pray arises from the knowledge that the one for whom prayer is being offered once attended Vigiles himself. Altogether about 140 men have left St. John's to serve overseas, and their names, together with country of service and date of departure, are recorded on two boards in the Common Room. What stories those boards could tell of Johnians who have played their part in spreading the gospel from Poland to Panama, from Rumania to Ruanda, to the Arctic and the Amazon! What of Dominque de Villega, who went to South America in 1881, and Lo Shukai and Chau Kwan-Lam, who early in this century returned to their native China as Johnians? What would these boards reveal of bishops and arch-deacons, of pastors and teachers—yes, and of a dentist and a naval lieutenant! We shall now turn to some of those who have gone from the College, whose names are here recorded, and briefly recall with thankfulness their service for the Kingdom of God overseas.

Of the naval lieutenant, we have a great story of pioneer missionary endeavour, for George Shergold Smith was one of the first from the College to serve in Africa. In 1875 the Church Missionary Society had felt compelled to respond to the challenge of the explorers Speke and Stanley, and send a mission to Uganda. Encouraged by an anonymous donation of £5,000 for the purpose, the Committee decided to appeal for men and money for its Nyanza mission. The first suitable offer of service linked together East and West Africa in a remarkable way. When in 1822 the little slave boy who became Bishop Crowther was rescued by H.M.S. *Myrmidon* off the coast of the Niger Delta, there was a midshipman on board who became Captain Shergold Smith, R.N. In due course, his son, George, went into the Navy and served in the Ashanti campaign of 1873-4. But fever affected his eyesight, causing him to leave the Service. He entered St.

John's Hall with a view to ordination, but his sight improved, and his heart went out to the people of Africa. "Send me out," he wrote to the C.M.S., "in any capacity; I am willing to take the lowest place." But as soon as he was accepted and began to share in the preparations for the new venture, he displayed such competence and efficiency that the Committee had no hesitation in appointing him leader of the expedition which included among its other members the Scottish engineer, Alexander Mackay, the Rev. C. T. Wilson, T. O'Neill, a vigorous Irishman and diocesan architect of Cork, two mechanics, G. J. Clark and W. M. Robertson, James Robertson, builder and agriculturist, and as medical director Dr. John Smith of Edinburgh. Fully appreciating the difficulties and dangers that lay before them, members of the party left in 1876.

The story of their work is well known.[1] Landing at Zanzibar, the expedition began the long trek up country, and soon their numbers were reduced from eight to five by ill-health. "We are yet (like Gideon's army) *too many*," wrote Shergold Smith on sending back Mackay, but the remaining four pressed forward. The two Smiths had a particularly trying time, for they were attacked by fever and dysentery, and all their porters deserted them. Dr. Smith died of fever on May 11th, 1877, being buried on the shores of Lake Nyanza. But the courage of the remaining three never failed. Towards the end of June a message arrived from king Mtesa urging them to come quickly to visit him, whereupon it was resolved that Shergold Smith and Wilson should go straight to Uganda. Landing on a small island, they were attacked by poisoned arrows, one of which carried a piece of his broken glasses into Smith's eye, destroying the sight. Wounded as he was, however, he sucked the poison from a wound in Wilson's shoulder, undoubtedly saving his life.

On July 2nd the King received them, and the first public Christian service held in Uganda took place in the King's compound on January 8th, Shergold Smith then left Wilson and crossed Lake Nyanza to help O'Neill bring over the heavy goods. Some months later they offered protection to an Arab trader who had quarrelled with a local King, Lukongeh. His men in retaliation surrounded the mission camp, and, probably on December 13th, 1877, massacred almost the whole party, including Smith and O'Neill. A few days before his death Smith had written: "Pray for us all, that we may know Him better and better until the perfect day. . . . We ask prayer that our hopes, our aims, our desires,

[1] E. Stock, *History of the Church Missionary Society*, iii. pp. 97-104.

may be one—the glorification of our Lord Jesus Christ, and the hastening of His kingdom." So "in a short time he fulfilled a long time," and his work was done. In proud and thankful remembrance of him, the College founded a prize, which is still awarded for an essay on missionary endeavour.

The College's first bishop was also a missionary, and one of the outstanding Evangelical leaders of his day. John Taylor Smith was a North Countryman, born at Kendal in 1860. At the age of twelve, he underwent a deep spiritual experience, a consciousness of pardon and release following upon a profound conviction of sin. After leaving Kendal Grammar School, he entered the family jewellery business, at the same time helping in local evangelistic work. Before long he became convinced that he was called to the ministry, and he entered St. John's Hall under Dr. Boultbee's Principalship in 1882. His time at college made a lasting impression upon him; as he realised the importance of this training period, he placed over his mantelpiece a card with four words on it; "As now, so then," to remind him that habits formed in College days would endure into ministerial life. He was ordained to the curacy of St. Paul's, Upper Norwood, and quickly made his mark by his work among men and boys. But wider horizons beckoned to him, and in 1890 he accepted the invitation of Bishop Ingham to serve as Canon Missioner in Sierra Leone. Here he was particularly successful, according to *The Times* obituary notice, "in procuring African volunteers for missionary work, and he had a marked influence on the younger British residents."

A turning-point in his life came while he was serving as a chaplain to the Ashanti expedition of 1895, for he was called upon to minister to the dying Prince Henry of Battenburg, who entrusted him with private messages for Queen Victoria and Princess Beatrice. So began a long connection with the Royal Family. Taylor Smith was soon made a Chaplain to the Queen, and in 1897, when Bishop Ingham retired, on the nomination of Archbishop Frederick Temple he was consecrated Bishop of Sierra Leone. Among the many who rejoiced at this appointment were the members of his old College, who at a special ceremony presented him with his episcopal robes. But direct missionary service was not to claim him much longer, for in 1901 he was offered by Lord Midleton, and accepted, the post of Chaplain-General to the Forces. This caused some criticism, especially among those who had given long service as chaplains, but in time he succeeded in gaining general respect. The outbreak of war in 1914 threw great responsibilities upon him owing to the rapid expansion of his department, but he continued to exercise great care in the selection of chaplains, always trying to pick men who had definite spiritual qualities. He was accused of choosing only men of Evangelical views, but this was not the case for, provided he was persuaded that an Anglo-Catholic had a definite spiritual message, he would feel quite happy in giving him an appointment. To quote *The Times* once again:

> "He showed great energy, coupled with a quiet determination to have his own way in certain matters. Having himself become less and less of a Protestant partisan, he refused to allow the churchmanship of certain Christian societies working in the Army to override his own desire to avoid extremes of any sort, and threw himself into the effort to unite the men of all ranks on the broader basis of the Church of England Men's Society. Nor should his care in bringing together, for advice and exchange of experiences, the chaplains commissioned to the Territorial Forces be forgotten."

When he reached retiring age in 1925, he was able to devote himself to those definitely Evangelical interests which always lay nearest to his heart, in particular the Children's Special Service Mission and the Keswick Convention, at which he was a frequent and much-beloved speaker. Neither was his old College forgotten. He used to preach about once a year, and was always assured of a tremendous welcome and send-off at the gate. Though asked on numerous occasions to join the College Council, he refused at first because of his many commitments, and in later years because he was so often absent abroad. He was a natural leader, and his broad figure and deep and kindly voice made those who met him long remember him and his words. He had a gift for pungent phrases, and some of his "best thoughts" still spring to mind: "Beware of the barrenness of a busy life"; "we are called to feed the sheep, not to amuse the goats." He seldom pronounced a blessing without the prayer that God would grant "increasingly and unceasingly the realisation of His pardon, His peace, His power, His wisdom, His humour, His strength, now and for evermore."

He travelled widely in his latter years, and then as always, he took every opportunity of speaking personally and with complete frankness to all whom he met on spiritual matters. When a high-ranking officer once said bluntly, "You know, I am not a religious man," he was told with equal bluntness, "Then, sir, you are not all there!" The Bishop always maintained the habit, begun in early years, of keeping the "morning watch" in prayer, by which means he kept free from the petty irritations of everyday life with a calm and serene manner indicative of inward peace. He was a great believer in physical fitness, and kept up his daily exercises until almost the end of his life. Awarded the C.V.O. in 1906, the C.B. in 1921 and the K.C.B. in 1925, he took all honours with his accustomed humility. He was unmarried, but his love of children and acceptance by them brought him much pleasure and many conversations which his young hearers never forgot. His sudden death at sea, when returning in March, 1938, from a voyage to Australia, brought sorrow to many, coupled with thanksgiving for all that God had been enabled to do through His servant.

Another great missionary bishop and contemporary of Taylor Smith was Llewellyn Henry Gwynne. Born of godly parents in June, 1863, near Swansea, the fifth of eight children, he went to Swansea Grammar School, and later developed into a notable footballer, playing centre-forward for Derby County. He entered St. John's Hall to train for the ministry in 1883, and was ordained to St. Chad's, Derby, in 1886. There followed a curacy and incumbency at Nottingham, but he never forgot an interest, awakened in his student days, in the life and work of General Gordon in the Sudan. It was accordingly no surprise to his friends when he offered to the Church Missionary Society, and in 1899 left to serve in that country. On arrival at Cairo, however, he was at first refused permission to proceed to Khartoum owing to the unsettled conditions in the area, but managed to arrive at Halfaya just before Christmas. With the full support of the Army authorities, he conducted the first Church of England service ever to take place at Omdurman on Christmas Day, 1889. This was held in what had been the Khalifa's harem, and the room was crowded, with Colonel Fergusson playing the small harmonium which Gwynne had brought with him. Neither Lord Cromer nor Kitchener would allow him to commence missionary work in the southern Sudan, so Gwynne had to be content to work as chaplain to the British personnel in the Egyptian Army, with small-scale contacts among Copts and Abyssinians, and after his busy life at Derby and Nottingham, he found this comparative inactivity most distasteful.

At length, in 1902, Gwynne received permission from Lord Cromer to open schools in Khartoum on behalf of the C.M.S. This, however, he regarded as only a beginning. The opportunity to open a mission station in the south for which he had striven so hard occurred in the autumn of 1905, when a capable team of C.M.S. missionaries set out, and linked up with Dr. Albert Cook, who had marched northward from Uganda, to found the new station at Malek among the Dinka people. He subsequently made many journeys throughout his vast parish, on one occasion at Port Sudan helping a side of very tough labourers engaged in building the port to win a local cricket match by taking several wickets, and then scoring 83. "I shall never forget it," he wrote. "I seemed to surpass myself and hit boundary after boundary, feeling as if I was hitting for the glory of God." There was a large congregation the following Sunday, and before long the Government had put up a wooden church at which weekly services were taken by the Governor of the province. In 1908 Gwynne was consecrated Suffragan Bishop of Khartoum, the Sudan at that time being part of the Diocese of Jerusalem.

When the First World War began, he offered his services as a chaplain, and in 1915 became deputy Chaplain-General in France, a post which he filled with great distinction. He was frequently up at the front, welcomed by officers and men alike as a personal friend. Indeed, the whole Chaplains' Department was strengthened by his service in France, while his old College friend, Bishop Taylor Smith, in Whitehall knew full well the value of his work. He organised what he called a chaplains' "bombing school," to Lord Plumer's amazement, meaning refresher courses for padres, and a retreat house was opened in 1917 at St. Omer, with B. K. Cunningham as Warden. Long afterwards Dean Inge recorded that Dr. Thorold, a subsequent Chaplain-General, was asked by Lord Plumer to name the man who did most to win the war. Thorold did not know, but Plumer replied: "I will tell you— Bishop Gwynne."[1]

It was generally assumed that he would become the new Chaplain-General, but Gwynne refused to allow his name to go forward. His heart was in the Sudan, and in 1920, on the division of the Jerusalem Diocese, he was appointed the first Bishop in Egypt and the Sudan. His return was hailed with delight by British, Greeks and Sudanese, and he received a resounding welcome to his old home at Khartoum. For the next twenty-five years he carried on his episcopal work over an area extending from the borders of Uganda to the Mediterranean. His favourite mode of travel was by air, and when the R.A.F. received orders from home that civilians were not to be carried in military aircraft, an exception was made in the case of the Bishop, who continued to fly across the 2,000 miles of his diocese until he was eighty

[1] *Diary of a Dean*, February 19th, 1934. Quoted, H. C. Jackson, *Pastor on the Nile*, p. 169.

years of age. It is difficult to over-emphasise the influence of the Bishop on the life of the Sudan. As *The Times* wrote of him (December 4th, 1957): "In an administration with moral and ethical standards as high as any in the British Empire, the life and character of the Bishop must be classed as one of its main contributory factors.... The Cathedral in Khartoum is a permanent memorial to the man who gave his life for the service of God in the Sudan." In a notable tribute in the same newspaper, Field-Marshal Lord Wilson wrote:

"During the dark days of June, 1940 ... things were very difficult for those serving in Cairo, as our country was regarded by both Egyptians and foreigners as beaten. At the time the sermons by the Bishop at evening service in the cathedral were a source of strength, courage and inspiration to all who heard them. ... The result was that evening services at the Cathedral became full of Service men, even to overflowing. The same continued during the times of crisis in the Middle East as the war fluctuated during the years 1941 and 1942. In the summer of 1943 the Bishop celebrated his eightieth birthday. The expressions of esteem and veneration on that day bore witness to what his congregation owed to him for his guidance during those days of stress."

Gwynne had immense moral courage and iron self-discipline, coupled with his strong Evangelical convictions. He could refuse to sign King Farouk's visiting book as a protest against his private life, and talk very directly with political and military leaders. Archbishop Lord Fisher has described him as "a great saint and a great hero of the Church," adding; "the secret of his life was that his only purpose was to capture [all men] for God as he himself was captured by God, body and soul." He was made a C.M.G. in 1917 and a C.B.E. in 1919. After his retirement from Egypt in 1946, he deeply appreciated the invitation to return in 1951 and dedicate a memorial window in Cairo Cathedral in memory of the Eighth Army, in the presence of Lord Montgomery, admirals, field-marshals, and marshals of the Royal Air Force, and a vast congregation. This was the climax of his long service to Egypt and the Sudan. He laid the foundation stone of his old College at its new home in Northwood, in 1955, as already related, and a month or two before he died preached on Battle of Britain Sunday to some 500 men of his local R.A.F. station. He was always a "fighting" man, but always beloved—a dauntless Christian warrior, yet a man of peace. His old College is proud to count him among her most distinguished sons.

If Africa was the scene of work for Taylor Smith and Gwynne, China claimed the service of two others who became bishops, Frank Houghton and K. G. Bevan. Bishop Frank Houghton, Senior Student of the College in 1917, was ordained that year to the curacy of St. Benedict, Everton, Liverpool. In 1920 he offered to the China Inland Mission, and sailed in November of that year. He served in the Diocese of West China for six years, for part of that time in charge of a boys' school, and for the last two years at the cathedral city of Paoning as Principal of a small Theological School. Owing to political unrest, he and his wife (a daughter of Bishop Cassels, who was one of the "Cambridge Seven") were unable to return to China when their furlough ended, and Mr. Houghton went temporarily as curate to the Rev. Barclay Buxton at Holy Trinity, Tunbridge Wells, until his appointment in 1928 as Editorial Secretary of the C.I.M. He and his wife returned to China in 1934, and spent most of the following year in touring throughout the country.

Then in 1936, Bishop Holden, who had succeeded Bishop Mowll on his translation to Sydney, suggested that the over-large Diocese of Eastern Szechawn (staffed, as far as missionaries were concerned, by members of the C.I.M. and a few members of the Bible Churchman's Missionary Society) and Western Szechwan (staffed by members of C.M.S.) should be divided. "I was staggered," writes Bishop Houghton, "by the suggestion that I should be appointed bishop of the eastern section." After much consideration and discussion, he consented to the proposal, and on St. Paul's Day, 1937, he was consecrated by Bishop Norris of North China, Bishop Holden, and two Chinese bishops. He served the Diocese of Eastern Szechwan for rather less than four years, for in October, 1940, he was appointed General Director of the China Inland Mission, based in Shanghai, though he still remained a member of the House of Bishops in China. He continued as Director until 1951, travelling widely in China, and also visiting the United States, Australia and New Zealand, Canada and South Africa on behalf of the Mission. After spending a few months in Dohnavar, South India, writing a notable biography of Miss Amy Carmichael, he returned to England as Vicar of St. Mark's, Leamington Spa, until, in January, 1960, he accepted the smaller charge of Drayton St. Peter, near Banbury.

Bishop Houghton's brother, A. T., also a Johnian, after some years as a B.C.M.S. missionary in Burma, was nominated Assistant Bishop of Rangoon. On his way out to be consecrated in Burma in March, 1941, however, his ship was attacked from the air, set on fire, and sunk. On arrival back in England, the Bishop of Rangoon decided that it would be too great a risk for Mr. Houghton to try to reach Burma again. For several years, therefore, he visited British universities under the auspices of the Inter-Varsity Fellowship to stir up missionary interest, until in 1945 he accepted the post of General Secretary of the Bible Church-man's Missionary Society, which position he still holds. He has been Chairman of the Keswick Convention Council since 1952.

Bishop Bevan was the sixth son of the Rev. J. A. Bevan, another Old Johnian, who was for over thirty years Vicar of St. George's, Great Yarmouth. The Bishop served in the Army for two years during the First World War before coming to Highbury from 1920 to 1923. After a curacy at Holy Trinity, Tunbridge Wells, he went out to China in 1925, arriving at a time of great change both in the country and in the status of the Church and of the missionaries serving it. In consequence, the younger missionaries found it much easier to make friends on equal terms with Chinese Christians, unhampered by the prestige which in former years automatically attached to Western Christian leaders. After fifteen years of pastoral and evangelistic work in a very large country area in Eastern Szechwan, he was consecrated Bishop of that Diocese in Shanghai Cathedral in October, 1940, in succession to his fellow-Johnian, Frank Houghton.

> "It was now," he writes, "that the vision of the Church which I had received at College became so valuable. There had been considerable development over the years in the progress of the Church towards self-government, and my particular task was to carry that through to the end, and see it achieved as quickly as possible. The decade from 1940 to 1950 was one of very great difficulty, with war, revolution and inflation. After the Communists had taken over control of China, the work of missionaries gradually came to an end. . . . My successor, Ts'ai fuh-ts'u, was consecrated in 1950. Though it was a great joy to see the fulfilment of our task in the handing over of leader-ship to a Chinese Bishop and one who had been so great a friend, it was sad to say goodbye the following year, knowing that we should get no further direct news of them."

Since 1951, Bishop Bevan has been Vicar of Woolhope in Hereford-shire, being appointed a Prebendary of Hereford Cathedral in 1956.

Not only West Africa, Egypt and the Sudan, but East Africa also claims links with St. John's. The wheel has come full circle since Shergold Smith led that first expedition to Nyanza, for since 1953 Dr. Leslie Brown has been Bishop and is now Archbishop of Uganda. Ordained to a curacy in Portsmouth in 1935, he went out to India in 1938 under C.M.S., where he served for some fifteen years, broken by two short periods which he spent as chaplain of Downing College and of Jesus College, Cambridge. His work has included experience of a varied kind: an English working-class parish, an outcast parish of people living near starvation level in south India, an Anglo-Indian mixed-race parish in Lahore, Pakistan, and as chaplain of a European community in Trivandrum, as well as working in the Theological College. He writes:

"I suppose that, from one point of view, the most important things that I can look back on are the formation and building of the Kerala United Theological Seminary in Trivandrum, which was the first United College to be formed in south India between episcopal and non-episcopal traditions. The fellowship we had in that United College was one of the contributory causes to the eventual formation of the Church of South India. Then, when the Church of South India was formed, I was chaplain to the Bishop presiding at the inauguration, and then Recording Secretary of the first Synod, and had the very great interest of being put on to the Committee for further union discussions with Lutherans and Baptists. I was also convenor of the Liturgy Committee, and in that capacity drafted the C.S.I. liturgy."

On Bishop C. E. Stuart's resignation in 1952, Mr. Brown was appointed to succeed him as Bishop of Uganda, and was consecrated in January, 1953. In 1957 the Bishop, who already held the London degrees of B.D. and M.Th., was awarded the London D.D. for his book, *The Indian Christians of St. Thomas*—the first Johnian student to obtain this degree, though it had previously been awarded to two members of the College staff.

"In Uganda" writes Dr. Brown, "it has been tremendous joy helping the development of the Church to a Province, and in carving up my own diocese; also, through suffragan areas, giving assistant bishops experience so that when they became diocesan bishops, there was really nobody who noticed the take-over, it was so smooth and efficient."

So the words of the College motto are still fulfilled in the lives of those working in the mission field today, as in the earlier years of its history.

Another contemporary Archbishop, working in a very different area, also received his early training at St. John's. Not himself a missionary, though the son of C.M.S. missionaries, Hugh Gough was born in India, and educated at Weymouth College and Trinity College, Cambridge, where he took over the Presidency of the Cambridge Inter-Collegiate Christian Union in 1926 at a time of crisis in its affairs, and immediately showed gifts of leadership and discernment. His time at Highbury under Dr. Gilbert was followed by ordination to the curacy of St. Mary, Islington, under Prebendary Hinde, and while here, he married in 1929 the daughter of Lord Kinnaird. After incumbencies in Bath and Carlisle, he came back to London as Vicar of St. Matthew's, Bayswater, from 1939 to 1946, but as a Territorial Army chaplain he was called up in 1939. He went overseas in 1942 as Chaplain to the 7th Battalion of the Rifle Brigade in the Western Desert, being wounded at the Battle of El Alamein. He was afterwards with the First Armoured Division in Tunisia, and from 1943 to 1945 was Deputy Assistant Chaplain-General with the 10th Corps in Italy. He was mentioned in despatches, and was awarded the O.B.E. in 1945. He returned to parochial work as Vicar and Rural Dean of his old parish, Islington, in 1946, and was made a Prebendary of St. Paul's in 1948. In this same year he accepted the invitation of Bishop H. A. Wilson of Chelmsford to become Suffragan Bishop of Barking and Archdeacon of West Ham. The work for which he became most widely known while holding this appointment was his service as Chairman of the Dr. Billy Graham Crusade in London in 1954-5 at Harringay and Wembley. The widespread interest aroused by this campaign made Bishop Gough's name well known throughout the country and in wider circles as an Evangelical leader, and he made a deep impression during a visit to Australia. When, therefore, Archbishop Mowll of Sydney died in 1958, it was not altogether surprising that Bishop Gough was elected to succeed him. There was general satisfaction when he was also elected Primate of Australia in 1959, and re-elected to that office under the new constitution in 1962. He had maintained a close connection with his old College through membership of the Council, and remains a valued friend.

The College's contribution to Church life in the Western Hemisphere should also be remembered through the work of three former Vice-Principals now serving in Canada: S. C. Steer as Bishop of Saskatoon and R. S. Dean as Bishop of Cariboo, while F. H. W. Crabb, after missionary work in the Sudan, as already mentioned, is now Principal of Emmanuel College, Saskatoon, both these bishops being his immediate predecessors at Emmanuel.

Others too numerous to mention have given many years of faithful service to the Church overseas, and as the College prepares to celebrate its centenary, it can look back and look around on those who through faith have subdued evil kingdoms in the hearts of men and women, "out of weakness were made strong, waxed valiant in fight" during countless unknown battles against cold and heat, doubt and temptation, weariness and discouragement among straw-thatched mud huts or desert heat, amid the poverty and dirt of vast townships, amid sickness and disease. Let one who was Senior Student in 1927, and who served a total of forty years in the Niger Diocese (for thirteen years as a layman) F. E. Wilcock, speak for the rest. As he left the College to commence his ordained ministry he wrote:

"Did you ever notice those idols that stand in my study? This time last year they stood in native huts away in West Africa. Why aren't they there now? Because their owners had the gospel preached to them in the power of the Holy Ghost, and they cast their idols away and looked unto Him and were lightened. Those idols represented a father's, a husband's, a young man's refuge, and help in trouble and source of blessing. Not many months ago I strolled away from my camp and stood still under the stars. A variety of sounds reminded me that I was surrounded by the town, where hundreds of simple natives lived in a darker spiritual shadow, their huts clustering among the trees. I and the three or four converts with me were the only ones in that town who could act as the link between His glorious light and their gross darkness. What an honour and what a privilege to be God's messenger of good tidings to them! If I cannot shine at the College examinations, if I cannot excel at the College athletics, at least let me be worthy of the College motto— 'Woe is unto me if I preach not the Gospel.'"

Those words, written in 1927, find their echo nineteen years later in the College magazine of 1946. Here a report is given of a paper by the same writer, now Archdeacon of Onitsha, and his closing remarks strike the same powerful note of optimism as those of the earlier year:

"When Bishop Crowther first landed in Onitsha in 1857, he found himself in a land of unrelieved darkness; the darkness of heathen customs and superstitions. Cannibalism, human sacrifice, head-hunting, burying alive and twin murder were practices which obtained all over the country. For the most part these have passed away and in their stead has risen up a young and virile Church. Surely the God who called her out of such darkness can enable her to fulfil her destiny now! She cannot, however, do it without the help of her elder brothers and sisters in this country. She does not beg for patronage, but for the right hand of fellowship expressed in prayer and lives dedicated to the service of God amongst the Africans."

It will be noticed that the same theme runs through these two extracts from the pen of the same writer, though separated by an interval of almost twenty years—the transition from darkness to light by the power of the gospel of Christ. Here is the message which those entrusted with this Good News must ever proclaim; and those who have gone forth from St. John's in the past, today, and in the years to come, are thus linked together in a fellowship of common service and endeavour as they seek to fulfil the purpose for which they have been called, to lead men out of the kingdom of darkness, that they may be translated into the kingdom of His dear Son.

Epilogue

A STORY such as that of the foundation, development and later history of the London College of Divinity can be viewed purely as a record, but certain reflections are prompted by the events and personalities described as they bear upon general objectives in training men for the Ministry. It was the work of Dr. Boultbee which opened men's eyes to the fact that a largely untapped source of material existed from which recruits for the Ministry could be attracted. Although St. Bees' and St. Aidan's Colleges had been founded to cater for non-graduates, yet Boultbee saw that many more men could be drawn from such sources into the Anglican ministry, who by their gifts and experience could make a valuable contribution to the Church's life.

Shortage of clergy today has brought this same question once more before men's minds; if there is now no large, untapped source of material, yet many suggestions have been put forward for easing the present man-power deficiency. The permanent diaconate, "worker-priests," greater and more imaginative use of lay-readers, of deaconesses and of women workers, have all been duly canvassed and discussed in various quarters, but without deep conviction that the answer is to be found in any of these. It may well be that a solution lies in the full and most effective deployment of all existing man-power, together with a certain re-grouping of parishes, at least in country districts, as is being tried, for example, in Lincolnshire. Yet perhaps the greatest hope of increasing clerical man-power lies in every incumbent being alert to suggest, to encourage, and to foster a possible sense of vocation among the young men of his parish.

Such a calling will most frequently be suggested, in the first instance, not so much by what the parish clergyman will *say* as by the living example of their own incumbent at work; by the ministry of a man obviously in love with his job, and on fire with love for Christ. One bishop of a very different churchmanship to that represented by St. John's once stated that he had entered the ministry because of the faithful and conscientious pastoral work of a certain Old Johnian in a large and busy parish. The call to the ministry, like religion itself, is more often caught than taught, and a great responsibility rests upon all the parochial clergy in this respect. If there lies the most promising field of recruitment at the present time, then, as in so many other spheres of Christian service, how much depends upon the alertness and spiritual awareness of the individual!

A great deal of thought is similarly being given to training methods. Criticism is intermittently directed at the academic level against the General Ordination Examination, and against all college courses, with a resultant streamlining and adjustment here and there. The argument is raised that non-graduate colleges should be abolished, because with intellectual standards in general increasing, a university degree should be a prerequisite for all ordinands, in view of the fact that they may well be called to minister to congregations which include doctors, solicitors and other qualified professional men and women, who will expect their parish priests to be at least as conversant with their specialised field of knowledge as are other men in similar positions of leadership. This raises the further question as to whether, in this age of specialisation, an overall general training for the ministry is either possible or desirable. Can a single training period of two or three years, it may be asked, be regarded as adequate for a man who may be called upon to minister in a large industrial parish, a new housing estate, a couple of country villages, a residential district or in the changing conditions of a popular holiday resort? Such widely varying spheres of service demand equally varying qualities and techniques from the men who find themselves so placed.

The retort that varying conditions or financial considerations make a longer training period virtually impossible, is partially, but not wholly valid. Ways and means could be found for overcoming the difficulty, provided that there was a general conviction that a satisfactory programme of additional training had been evolved. There would probably be broad agreement that it is rather on the practical than on the academic side that training weaknesses are more apparent, and those engaged in teaching pastoral theology are acutely aware of this problem. Such activities as regular weekly teaching in Sunday schools and Bible classes, or reading the services with occasional opportunities to preach, together with vacation missions when teams of students engage in a series of meetings and services, with intensive parochial visiting, under the experienced supervision of members of the college staff, even when supplemented by visiting lecturers on specific subjects, are hardly sufficient as a basic preparation for parochial work. Yet how many colleges can offer much more than this? It has been suggested that the whole field of pastoral theology could well be left to the first curacy, with specially qualified examining chaplains to lecture and give practical supervision in the setting of the parochial ministry during the diaconate. While this might be possible in the case of the less busy parishes, it is doubtful whether it would prove universally practicable.

A twofold plea might be entered here: first, that one Long Vacation term should be spent by each ordinand in a parish, preferably not that to which he is going as curate, working with pay as a recognised member of the staff, being taken by the incumbent or curate to visit in homes and hospitals, factories, mines or shipyards and (if during term time) to schools. Where this has been tried, ordinands have expressed their gratitude for the value of such an experience. Secondly, it might be possible to suggest that a man should deliberately aim at gaining experience in different types of parish during his curacy days, and in particular that one curacy should be spent in attachment to a group of country parishes. It is probably true to say that the majority of ordinands today have little experience of country life, apart from the brief periods spent on holiday. To live and work in the country, however, is a very different matter, as the man who takes a country parish without such previous experience will quickly discover. Some earlier preparation for this during his curacy days would save him from making mistakes when he takes up a more responsible position. It will also introduce many to a completely new world, and incidentally do much to dispel their illusion that a country parish is suitable only for those who are approaching retirement age!

The London College of Divinity deals with men from a wide diversity of experience. A few are graduates, and some can take the courses for the London B.A. or B.D. It differs from every other college, except King's College, London, in being able to offer in the A.L.C.D. the additional attraction of a recognised diploma, which is of near "pass degree" standard, and the College is thus enabled to set its academic requirements for acceptance rather higher than some other non-graduate colleges. The Church as a whole, however, is realising today, not only as a matter of expediency, but as deliberate policy, the valuable contribution which can be made to her ministry by the "over 40's"; that is, by men who have had many years experience of industrial, business or professional employment. Such men can speak from inside knowledge on many matters touching on contemporary life, thus helping to bridge the gulf so constantly deplored between Church and people.

It may be questioned, however, whether such men are best prepared for the ministry in a general college setting. There is much to be said for more individual methods to be adopted; for seminars to be substituted for lectures, with much greater opportunity for discussion and for asking questions in small groups; for attention to be concentrated on essay writing and expression in clear and grammatical English rather than on passsing examinations; for a thorough knowledge of the text of the Bible, together with an understanding of the basic Christian doctrines; for a study of Church history dealing with the early period, the Reformation and the last 150 years, together with an elementary introduction to Christian ethics, with particular reference to modern social problems. Such a course, in the setting of regular daily worship provided in the cathedral cities, together with the necessary individual attention such as could be given by the residentiary canons and suitably qualified diocesan clergy, could well be extended to many different centres. The Worcester Training Course does, in fact, cover most of this ground, but a great deal would depend on the choice of a principal or superintendent.[1] Men for such work could be found, but many of them would welcome some training course for themselves before undertaking so exacting a task; yet this is not at present available. In this age of specialisation, the Church cannot expect to be free from corresponding pressures. There are obvious dangers in over-specialisation, but there is much to be said for more courses on particular aspects of ministerial life on the lines of that conducted, for example, by the College of Preachers, which has been deeply appreciated by those who have attended (the Director, the Rev. D. W. C. Ford, M.Th., was both a student and on the staff of St. John's), while the fact that it fills a recognised need is indicated by the numbers applying for future enrolment.

But when all has been said on training methods, and on the importance of fostering a sense of vocation for the Ministry among all who could make a useful contribution to the Church's life and work, there remains the fundamental significance of the message to be proclaimed, and the necessity to proclaim it in contemporary thought forms. In his vision for the future of the new St. John's, the Archbishop of York, while still Principal, could write:

[1] Here Worcester are highly fortunate in the expert guidance of Canon C. B. Armstrong.

The first [vision] is, obviously that [the College] should fulfil its primary function of sending out into the Ministry a stream of men whose hearts and minds God has touched by His spirit. I see them as men with an overpowering love of the Evangel, men with a deep loyalty to the Church of England, men with a world-view of the Church, men who at least are beginning to hold in balance (as do our Anglican formularies) the Ministry of Word and of Sacrament, men who have drunk deep enough at the wells of evangelism and of worship to know something of their inexhaustibility. Unless the College sends forth such men, her very *raison d'être* has ceased.[1]

Men of this calibre will indeed be evangelists as that term is defined by the *Archbishops' Committee of Enquiry into the Evangelistic Work of the Church*, which reported in 1918:[2]

> To evangelise is so to present Jesus Christ in the power of the Holy Spirit, that men shall come to put their trust in God through Him, to accept Him as their Saviour, and serve Him as their King in the fellowship of His Church.

At times there have been tensions in the College between the more conservative and liberal exponents of Evangelicalism, both at staff and student levels. But spiritual life flourished when the emphasis was placed rather on the content of the word "Evangelical" than on the "conservative" or "liberal" elements attached to it. Wherever Evangelical doctrine has been taught positively, and has not taken refuge in obscurantism or closed its eyes to the pursuit of new truth, it has always made its distinctive impact on the life of the Church of England by its stress on the prophetic ministry, on individual responsibility and on personal commitment.

What, then, it may be asked, is the "evangel" committed to our trust? In brief, the gospel is the good news that God is, and that God is love. Man has clearly reached a situation when the facts of sin and evil can hardly be queried; collectively and individually, he has departed from the path designed for him to travel, and is unable to recover himself. It is to such a situation as this that God has spoken by word and action. The life, death, and Resurrection of Jesus Christ, the Son of God, all played their part in reconciling man to the God from whom his own wilfulness had separated him; in St. Paul's words, "God was in Christ reconciling the world unto Himself."[3] God's initiative was essential to do for man what he could not begin to do for himself. Now by the work of the Holy Spirit, man is both brought to perceive

[1] *Johnian*, Michaelmas, 1950, p. 5.
[2] Quoted in *Towards the Conversion of England* (1945), para. 1.
[3] II Cor. v. 19.

the need of reconciliation, and also the means which God has provided for this to be effected through Christ. Man's response to this reconciling work is made through repentance and faith; repentance being not merely sorrow for sin, but a determination with divine help to put it away. Faith is not mere credulity, or intellectual assent to a series of facts, but an act of committal whereby (to use the vivid phrase of Bishop Brent) man is prepared "to swing his life between a risk and an opportunity" by taking God at His word, by claiming His forgiveness for all that is past, and then going forth to prove in experience the truth of that word in dependence upon the Holy Spirit to give the needed power for daily living, nourished by the ministry of Word and Sacrament, prayer and Bible study, and by the joy of ever-deepening Christian fellowship. A consciousness of inward peace enables the Christian to go on his way rejoicing, to work in the service of God and of his fellow-men.

This gospel is old, but relevant by the power of the living Christ to meet the needs of each generation; though rooted in past historic facts, it yet vitally concerns the issues confronting the world today, giving a strong foundation upon which a man can build his life to withstand the fears and frustrations, the doubts and pressures, the false creeds and false gods of this and every age. It enables a man to face the future not with foreboding, but with hope. "Ultimately, the evidence for the credibility of the Gospel in the eyes of the world will rest upon the evidence of a quality of life manifested in the Church which the world cannot find elsewhere."[1] Only in so far as a theological college continues to send forth men who manifest this quality of life will she fulfil her purpose of service to the Church today, and in the days to come.

> Through men whom worldlings count as fools
>   Chosen of God and not of man,
> Reared in Thy secret training schools
>   Moves forward Thine eternal plan.
>
> And now, though hidden from our ken
>   In Midian desert, Sinai's hill,
> Spirit of God, Thou hast Thy men,
>   Waiting Thy time to do Thy will.[2]

In this faith and hope is the early vision of Peache and Boultbee for St. John's Hall continually fulfilled.

[1] *Towards the Conversion of England*, para. 75.
[2] Quoted by kind permission of the author, the Right Rev. Frank Houghton.

Principal Sources

College Council Minute Books, 1879-1962.
College Magazine, 1868-1885 (19 vols.), in MS.
St. John's Magazine, 1885-1907 (6 vols.), in print.
The Johnian, 1907-1962 (9 vols., together with unbound copies).

Letters and Memoranda

The Archbishop of York (the Most Rev. and Right Hon. F. D. Coggan).
The Archbishop of Sydney (the Most Rev. Hugh Gough).
The Archbishop of Uganda (the Most Rev. Leslie Brown).
The Bishop of St. Edmundsbury and Ipswich (the Right Rev. A. H. Morris).
The Bishop of Cariboo (the Right Rev. R. S. Dean).
The Bishop of Saskatoon (the Right Rev. S. C. Steer).
The Bishop Suffragan of Stepney (the Right Rev. F. E. Lunt).
The Right Rev. K. G. Bevan.
The Right Rev. F. Houghton.
The Right Rev. T. Sherwood Jones.

The Rev. C. W. R. J. Anderson.
The Rev. Canon E. G. Bevan.
The Rev. W. G. Brown.
The Rev. F. S. Bull.
The Rev. D. W. Cleverely Ford.
The Rev. R. G. G. Hooper.
The Rev. O. A. C. Irwin.

The Rev. Hugh Jordan.
The Rev. R. H. P. King.
The Rev. Canon T. G. Mohan.
The Rev. Norman Motley.
The Rev. Canon A. W. Parsons.
The Rev. Martin Parsons.
The Rev. G. H. Stevens.
The Rev. Douglas Webster.
The Rev. D. C. St. V. Welander.
The Rev. Canon A. R. Winnett.

INDEX